5.⁰⁰

AF251901

SPORTING GUNS
An illustrated reference guide
for collectors

SPORTING GUNS

An illustrated reference guide for collectors

F. Wilkinson

ARMS AND ARMOUR PRESS

London Melbourne Harrisburg, Pa. Cape Town

Published in 1984 by Arms and Armour Press,
Lionel Leventhal Limited, 2-6 Hampstead High Street,
London NW3 1QQ.
Australasia: 4-12 Tattersalls Lane, Melbourne,
Victoria 3000.
USA: Cameron & Kelker Streets, P.O. Box 1831,
Harrisburg, Pa 17105.
South Africa: Sanso Centre, 8 Adderley Street,
P.O. Box 94, Cape Town 8000.

1 2 3 4 5 6 7 8 9 0

British Library Cataloguing in Publication Data:
Wilkinson, Frederick
Sporting guns
1. Shotguns–History I. Title
683.4′26′09 TS536.8
ISBN 0-85368-637-8

Printed in Great Britain

CONTENTS

INTRODUCTION

Primitive man was obliged to hunt in order to eat, but this necessity was largely removed as urban civilization developed. The instinct to hunt remained, however, and was then indulged as a sport. The hunter could catch his prey by two methods – by stealth, using snares and traps, or by hitting it from a distance. The latter method involved the use of such missiles as throwing-sticks, spears, stones or arrows. Until the fourteenth and fifteenth centuries these were the only means available to the hunter, but the discovery of gunpowder added a new weapon. The first firearm was crude, rather unreliable and often wildly inaccurate, but its use required less skill and certainly much less training than for the bow.

In early firearms the match (the tip of a length of smouldering cord) ignited a charge of gunpowder housed in the breech of the long barrel. These matchlock muskets were basic, but they were cheap, reliable, easy to make and easily maintained. Newer systems of igniting the powder were developed, but the trusty matchlock musket remained popular with poorer hunters until the early eighteenth century.

Early in the sixteenth century a newer, more sophisticated means of ignition was developed whereby the smouldering match was replaced by the wheel-lock. A small steel wheel, driven by a spring, rotated against a piece of sulphide mineral (pyrites), the resulting friction generating a shower of glowing sparks to ignite a small amount of powder, the priming. When the priming flared, in a pan situated next to the touchhole (a small hole which pierced the barrel), the flame passed through to ignite the main charge of powder which discharged the bullet. Obviously the wheel-lock was far more convenient than the old matchlock and was soon in demand by hunters although there was some opposition by such rulers as Maximilian I (1493–1519) who issued decrees condemning the new weapon. The very nature of its complex construction meant that the wheel-lock was expensive to produce and so was restricted to the wealthier groups. The weapons came to be regarded as status symbols and much money was spent on embellishing them. Leading artists produced designs for their decoration, and stocks, usually of walnut, were carved and inlaid with ivory, horn, mother-of-pearl, silver, gold and steel. Locks and barrels were chiselled into grotesque shapes or engraved with a wide range of hunting, classical and military motifs. The weapons often became works of art in their own right.

Beautiful they were, but accurate they were not, and to hit a moving target was a difficult task. The majority of hunters limited their skill to sitting targets, birds roosting or feeding. One obvious way to increase the chances of a hit was to substitute a number of small bullets for the single large one. These smaller projectiles, known as hail shot, tended to spread after leaving the muzzle, thereby increasing the potentially lethal area which, in turn, meant that careful aiming was not quite so important. This lack of precision in aiming was condemned by the authorities, since it encouraged shooting habits detrimental to the accuracy needed in war. It could well be that they were also concerned with the higher killing rate of hail shot.

Most wheel-lock weapons, both muskets and rifles, had a short stock which was held pressed against the cheek when aiming. Since the barrels were usually fairly thick and heavy, the kick or recoil produced by the burning powder was largely absorbed and caused little discomfort to the shooter. Many sporting wheel-locks were fitted with hair-triggers which required only the lightest touch to activate the mechanism. This meant that the shooter was far less likely to go off his aim than when he had to exert the fairly heavy pressure needed to operate the ordinary rather stiff trigger.

Trigger guards were usually contoured to provide a firm and easy grip for the fingers which were wrapped round the outside of the guard. The lock mechanism was mounted on a metal plate, the lock plate, which was usually set into a recess on the stock.

One group of wheel-locks which differed from the usual pattern were the light, elegant hunting rifles known as Tschinkes, the name deriving from the town of Teschen (now Cieszyn) in Bohemia, near the present Czech–Polish border. The stock of the Tschinke was usually slender with a strongly curved butt, and the lock had most of its mechanism mounted externally rather than fitted into the internal recess.

Although the wheel-lock was reliable and efficient it was expensive, it could jam and any mechanical malfunction could be difficult to repair for all but the most skilled craftsmen. Later in the sixteenth century a simpler means of generating sparks was being developed. The rotating grooved wheel was replaced by a metal arm gripping a small piece of flint between two metal jaws. The arm was so placed that as it swung forward and down, the shaped piece of flint was scraped down a metal plate to produce a shower of sparks which fell into the pan filled with priming powder. The power was supplied by a strong V-spring which pressed against the tumbler, a metal block to which the arm holding the flint (the cock) was attached. A sliding metal plate over the pan prevented rain or wind from disturbing the priming and prior to firing this plate had to be removed either manually or mechanically. As the flint swung forward and down it not only struck sparks, but also pushed the upright plate forward and out of the way. This snaphaunce (snaphance) mechanism did not achieve very wide usage for it was soon improved upon and became the flintlock. The upright steel plate and the pan cover were united in a single L-shaped piece of metal, pivoted at the tip of the base, known to collectors as the frizzen. By this simple means the need for opening the pan cover was removed, for it was done automatically, the moving cock pushing the frizzen forward to expose the priming.

By the mid seventeenth century most sporting guns were fitted with a flintlock and had very long barrels. The length of barrel was dictated by the uncertain nature of the powder; it was slow burning, and in order to impart maximum energy to the missile it was important that it remain inside the barrel until all or most of the powder had burned. As the quality of powder improved, barrels were shortened. Stock shape was modified in the light of experience, and by the middle of the century the gun could be held against the shoulder, which facilitated aiming.

More and more shooters turned to 'shooting flying' and were able to take the birds on the wing. In order to give them as much chance as possible of hitting their target, gunmakers began to produce double-barrelled guns with two separate barrels mounted on the stock. As technical skill improved the gunmaker was able to unite the barrels into a single unit, joined by a rib along the centre. Most barrels were arranged side by side with a separate lock for each, but some were fitted one above the other (over and under). Many of these used only one lock, and the barrels could be rotated to bring each in line with the lock for firing. British shooters seemed rather reluctant to adopt the double-barrelled gun, but by late in the eighteenth century well known gunmakers such as Egg, Manton, Parker and others were producing very fine double-barrelled flintlock guns.

Loading these early guns was a slow business: powder, then wads and then shot each had to be poured down the barrel and rammed home with the ramrod. Many attempts were made to simplify the loading sequence, mainly in the development of guns which could be loaded at the breech. Barrels were so made that they could be pivoted to give access to the breech; others devised systems wherein only the breech opened. Some early systems used a small, reloadable, metal cylinder which was inserted into the breech, but these and almost all other systems suffered from poor sealing at the breech. This meant that burning gas and powder could erupt into the shooter's face, and the force exerted on the shot or bullet was reduced.

The flintlock sporting gun was generally plainer than the wheel-lock, but most have a pleasing look and balance, usually with a barrel about 30 inches in length. British sporting guns were generally plainer than those by Continental makers who embellished the weapon with carving, inlay and chiselled metal work.

Pans were so shaped as to make the priming less vulnerable to rain and damp, friction was reduced by the use of rollers and breeches were shaped so as to improve ignition. Corrosion by the burning priming powder was reduced by lining the pan and vent with gold or platinum, and by the early nineteenth century the sportsman had a well made, efficient sporting gun.

There were still problems inherent in the flintlock system, and for the hunter the hangfire and priming flash were the most irritating. From the moment when the trigger was pressed a sequence of events, each quite short, combined to produce an appreciable delay: the cock swung forward striking sparks which fell into the priming, this flared and the flash passed through the touchhole and finally ignited the main charge. This delay – the hangfire – meant that the shooter had to compensate for it when aiming at a moving target. Another small but irritating problem was the flash of the priming which preceded the shot, for this gave a brief warning to the quarry.

Both problems were overcome by the efforts of a Scottish clergyman, Alexander Forsyth, who devised a means of dispensing with the priming completely. In 1807 he patented the idea of using the flash produced by the detonation of chemicals known as fulminates. A tiny amount of fulminate was placed over the touchhole or vent and detonated by a blow from a solid-nosed hammer; the resultant flash was directed into the breech to fire the main charge. Forsyth set up a shop in London and produced a range of firearms using his percussion system. On the early guns the fulminate was packaged in small paper capsules, pieces of quill, rolled into pills or dispensed from special containers, but by the 1820s copper percussion caps had replaced virtually all other systems. The little copper thimble had a small amount of fulminate deposited on the inside top surface and was placed on the top of a small metal pillar (the nipple), through which a tiny hole was drilled to the breech. Hangfire was greatly reduced and the flash from priming completely eliminated.

Apart from the obvious advantages of this new system there was one other which appealed to the canny shooter – his old flintlock gun could easily be converted to the new system. Pan, frizzen and spring were removed from the lockplate and a hammer was substituted for the cock, while the internal mechanism remained untouched. A plug with attached nipple was fitted into the touchhole and the gun was ready for action.

Although the new percussion system was a great step forward, the sporting gun had changed little from the seventeenth century in that it was still loaded from the muzzle. Paper cartridges, containing a charge of powder and the bullet, had been developed as long ago as the sixteenth century. The end was torn open and a pinch of powder was placed in the priming pan and the cover was closed. The remaining powder, paper and bullet were tipped down the barrel and rammed home with the ramrod. As early as 1812, Samuel Johannes Pauly had designed a very satisfactory breech-loading gun which used a cartridge with a metal base. In the centre of the base was set a pellet of fulminate, while the body held a charge of powder and the bullet or shot. The barrels of Pauly's gun were movable and the cartridge could be loaded directly into the open breech; the barrels were closed and an enclosed striker hit and detonated the fulminate. The metal base expanded slightly so sealing the breech and ensuring a minimum escape of gas. The gun was then opened, the metal base was removed and a fresh cartridge loaded. Despite its apparent advantages, however, the Pauly gun was never developed.

In 1832 a Frenchman, Casimir Lefaucheux, patented a breech-loading gun the barrels of which could be unlocked and lowered to allow a self-contained, paper cartridge to be loaded into the breech. A small tail at the rear of the cartridge contained the fulminate which was struck by the hammer to detonate the charge. In 1835 he further developed the idea and produced the pinfire cartridge. This consisted of a cardboard tube holding the charge and shot, but embedded at the base was a small capsule of fulminate. One end of a small metal rod or pin touched the fulminate while the other end projected through the case. When the cartridge was loaded into the breech the end of the rod projected through a small slot cut into the top of the breech. When the trigger was pressed the hammer fell and hit the pin forcing it down to detonate the fulminate.

The pinfire cartridge was a step forward, but it was vulnerable to accidental discharge. In 1855 another French patent by Pottet introduced what was in effect the immediate ancestor of the modern shotgun shell, the centrefire cartridge. Further development by British designers meant that by the 1860s the shooter was equipped with an efficient breech-loading sporting gun.

Hammer Guns

It was not easy to convert a percussion-cap gun to either pinfire or centrefire, and the new guns were of the type known as hammer guns. The barrels system might vary, but the action or firing mechanism was fairly standard: two small spring-loaded pins set at such an angle that when struck by a side-mounted hammer they would drive forward and down to hit the centre-mounted cap in the base of the cartridge. The hammers were rather vulnerable to knocks which could cause an accidental discharge. On the other hand it was very easy to see when the gun was cocked for the hammers had to be pulled back to an upright position before pressing the trigger. Despite their disadvantages hammer guns remained popular long after they had been made obsolete by technical advances. Many hammer guns are unsafe for use with modern cartridges because they were designed to cope with black or gunpowder and modern nitro powders develop pressures too great for the breech to cope with.

Hammerless Guns

Gunmakers were soon trying to produce a gun which did not require external hammers, but which had a striker enclosed within the body of the gun. As early as 1862 a patent for such an action was granted but was not generally adopted. In 1871, T. Murcott patented a hammerless action which was cocked, i.e. made ready to fire, by pressing down on a lever situated around the trigger guard. Allport developed another action cocked by rotating an under-lever which was also set around the trigger guard. Other makers produced actions which were operated by a top lever set above the stock; movement of the lever unlocked the barrels and their weight was used to help cock the action – a popular make was the 'Club' by the firm of W. W. Greener. By far the most popular action was that patented in 1875 by Anson and Deeley, two employees of the firm of Westley Richards. When the barrels were dropped two levers compressed the main springs to cock the action. This system was modified by other gunmakers such as Purdey and Greener.

The Anson–Deeley type action can be mounted in a gun in two main ways. The method used on cheaper guns is known as the box lock in which the action is set into a box area in the metal body of the gun. The other method of fitting is known as a side lock and here the mechanism is mounted on separate plates and then fitted into the action of the gun and the head of the stock. A variation is the back-action side lock which has the mainspring mounted behind the side lock instead of in the more usual position in front. The hammerless lock mechanism enabled designers to produce a number of new types of gun.

Pump Action

Guns of this design have a magazine, usually mounted below the barrel, loaded with a number of cartridges. The fore-end is attached to an internal mechanism and as it is pushed backwards and forwards a cartridge is extracted from the magazine, lifted and loaded into the breech. After this round has been fired, the fore-end is again operated and this time the empty case is ejected before the next round is loaded. One obvious advantage is the potentially more rapid rate of fire. The pump, slide or trombone action was introduced in 1892 by the well known Winchester Arms Company who had previously broken new ground in 1887 when they produced a shotgun with the famous lever action. The pump-action gun does have certain drawbacks such as weight and balance and it can be difficult maintaining an aim when operating the fairly heavy action. Its potentially high rate of fire has made it an ideal weapon for delivering many quick shots, and short-barrelled versions are much favoured by police and military in dangerous combat situations.

Automatic Shotguns

The principle of reloading mechanically was developed in 1905 when John Browning, one of the most important and prolific firearms designers, produced a self-loading gun. He used the force generated by the recoil to perform the functions of ejection and reloading. The advent of this new gun did not have any immediate marked effect, but during the 1920s and 1930s demand gradually increased and a number of good models became available. In 1955 an improved method, using some of the gas produced by the explosion to operate the system, was put on the market and although still received with suspicion by some shooters and excluded from some shooting events, automatic shotguns are gaining in popularity.

Bolt-Action Shotguns

A few models, especially in .410in, have been produced where the cartridge is loaded into the breech and secured by a bolt action very similar to that found on rifles. It is a slow and rather cumbersome system, however, and was never popular although often used on cheaper guns.

Punt Guns

These large guns were made with barrels from seven to nine feet long, having a bore of 1¼–1½ inches and weighing about 70–80 pounds. They were used by professional wildfowlers to ensure a large bag. Most were made with large trunnions and were mounted on low profile punts. Needham, a gunmaker, designed some guns of this kind, which used the same system of breech loading as he fitted to his shotguns, a form of needle fire with a bolt-like breech-block. Later, Snider actions were used, while Holland & Holland produced one on which the stock was lowered to give access to the breech. The heavy charge used in these guns necessitated some form of recoil absorption, either ropes or special springs.

Barrels

Obviously the barrel is of vital importance in any gun and much time and effort was, and still is, spent to produce a true barrel which shoots consistently and safely. Construction methods were aimed at making a barrel which was light, strong and hard wearing. Early barrels were built up of lengths of tubing, usually about six inches long, the ends of which were heated and forged together. A cheaper, but less reliable method involved the wrapping of a metal plate around a circular former; the edges being hammered and welded.

During the nineteenth century most sporting gun barrels were composed of a mixture of iron and steel known as Damascus. The metal was hammered out into rods which were then heated, twisted and hammered into a flat bar. Cheaper barrels were then made up by wrapping the bar spirally around a former and welding it into a tube. Barrels of better quality were made up of two, three or more bars, and it was generally agreed that three bars or 'tapes' were best. The composite tape was wound spirally around a mandril and the joins were heated and forged together; this process was repeated until the barrel-maker had a tube long enough for his needs. The thickness of the wall was carefully graded, being greatest at the breech.

During the 1880s, advances in metallurgy meant that barrels could now be made from steel and several systems were tried, but the most popular were made from 'Whitworth's fluid-compressed steel'. In general, steel barrels were equal to, if not better than, Damascus for strength, but they were generally lighter. The steel ingot produced by Whitworth's method was cut and rolled into 3-foot long bars or blanks. The barrel was then bored out to the appropriate size and this required three operations: a rough boring, followed by a fine boring, and finished off by lapping or lead-polishing. During the boring a skilled craftsman, the setter, was constantly checking to see that the barrel was straight and true – an operation performed entirely by eye.

When completed the barrel was prepared for 'putting together' to form a double-barrelled gun and to this end a shaped block of metal, approximately 2½in × 1in × ½in, the 'lump', was prepared. The two barrels, with the lump in position below the breech, were then brazed together at the breech and then soldered on the top and bottom.

Early barrels were cylindrically bored, but from the eighteenth century it was realised that if the internal diameter were slightly reduced near the muzzle the shot would be compressed into a smaller pattern and range would be slightly increased. This construction, known as the choke, was first patented in 1866 by an American, Roper, and shortly afterwards in Britain by William Pope; its superior performance was clearly demonstrated at a public trial in New York in 1873. In January 1875 another test in Birmingham showed similar results and thenceforward most guns had choke-bored barrels. The amount of constriction varies from about 5 to 50 thousandths of an inch, with degrees of choke described as true cylinder, improved cylinder, quarter, half and full – the maximum. The internal diameter of the barrel is the determining feature in defining its size or bore, ranging from 4 to 28 bore. The nomenclature is based on the old system of defining the bore of a gun by the weight of the bullet it fired; thus if a barrel fired a bullet weighing one ounce the gun was defined as a 16 bore because sixteen bullets weighed one pound – in a four bore each ball weighed four ounces. Today the majority of sporting guns are 12 bore, although 20 bore is gaining in popularity. One exception to this rule is that the smallest size is defined by the inside barrel diameter which is .410 of an inch.

On most double-barrelled guns the barrels are mounted side by side, but for some shooting the alternative one above the other system, 'over-and-under', is preferred.

Rifling
A few makes of shotgun, such as the Paradox, had the last four inches of the barrel cut with rifling grooves so that the gun could fire shot or a ball. Externally there was little difference, but in order to ensure greater accuracy when using ball ammunition, the sights were more elaborate.

Proof
The sale of guns in England was controlled by the London and Birmingham Companies until 1868, in which year an Act of Parliament set down a common scale of proof for both companies. The purpose of the proof, which had been employed in various forms almost since the first guns were made, was to ensure that the barrel was safe and would not burst when the gun was fired. If the barrels passed the tests set down by the Act of Parliament the barrel was stamped with a mark to show this. Similar systems were used in

other countries and as the conditions have varied so have the marks. The bibliography will indicate the relevant references for this information.

Stocks

The wooden part of the gun is of vital importance because a good gun must 'fit' the shooter if he is to shoot well. To achieve a fit, a 'try' gun is used on which the stock can be adjusted in various ways. The shooter uses the gun to fire at clay pigeons while carefully observed by the instructor who can see where any problems may arise. The stock is adjusted and the process repeated until the gun comes up automatically into the correct shooting position.

The stock and barrel are usually more or less in line, but for various reasons the shooter may want the deviation of stock and barrel to be greater. If the stock deviates to the right it is said to be 'cast-off', if to the left it is 'cast-on'. The cross-eyed stock is made for the shooter who, for some reason, holds the gun with the stock against his right shoulder but aims with his left eye.

Walnut is the most commonly used wood both for its strength and its beautiful grain pattern. In general, for weight, colour and vein, French walnut is thought best especially those pieces from near the junction of root and trunk.

Actions

Obviously there had to be some device which would allow the barrels to be moved for loading and this movement was also used to cock the locks, and for other purposes. That part of the gun which houses the locking and opening mechanism is known as the action.

Lefaucheux's opening action was operated by moving a lever mounted beneath the breech which unlocked the barrels and allowed them to drop. Other makers retained the idea of a lever, but mounted it on top of the action. Some makers mounted a side-lever and others made theirs encircle the trigger guard. Purdey's, a very famous firm, designed a system in which a short, thin lever was operated by the thumb pushing through an opening at the front of the trigger guard.

The majority of sporting guns had barrels which swung down, but Jeffries, a Norwich maker, made some guns with barrels that remained horizontal but pivoted sideways. His system never became popular and the vast majority of sporting guns use the dropping barrels.

When the gun was loaded it was essential that a safe, firm locking system held the barrels firmly against the breech. W. W. Greener, a British maker, used a cross bolt which engaged with a hole cut in a central rear projection set at the breech end of the barrels. Westley

Richards patented a system which replaced the usual rather long lever by a short thumb lever set between the hammers. This firm also developed the idea of the 'doll's head'. This was a short bar projecting from the top of the barrels. The bar had a rounded tip which engaged with a similar shaped recess at the breech.

Various improvements to the opening action of guns were made, such as the fitting of an extra spring which exerts a pressure on the barrels. These are known as 'self-openers'; when the lever is operated the spring pushes against the barrels so that they move without the need for the shooter to touch them. On some guns made by Purdey the mainspring itself provided the force to open the barrels, and on some the action is restricted and will only operate when the gun has not been fired. There are other variations known as 'easy-openers' and this term usually applies to guns on which the barrels are activated when only one cartridge has been fired.

It was not long before gunmakers began to utilise the leverage developed by the pivoting barrels to perform various extra functions. Most common was the cocking of the action by pushing back the tumblers to compress the mainsprings and lock the sears. Designs for this action were in use as early as the 1860s, although on many of the earlier patents it was the action of the lever which effected the cocking rather than the barrels. In the Anson and Deeley lock of 1875, the cocking was effected by a lever set in the action which was activated by the movement of the barrels.

Yet another refinement was the fitting of devices to facilitate removal of empty cartridge cases. The simplest was a small arm which, as the barrels were lowered, was pushed backwards lifting the rear of the case clear. A further improvement was the fitting of automatic, spring-operated ejectors which were sufficiently powerful to throw the empty case from the breech. The idea was first introduced by a Birmingham gunmaker, Needham, but was complicated by the necessity of extending the lump below the action. Greener and Lancaster both simplified and improved the action and today guns of the better quality are all fitted with ejectors which are so arranged that they only operate if the barrel has been fired. This is achieved by linking the ejector mechanism to the mainspring in such a way that a compressed, i.e. unfired, spring does not activate the mechanism.

Safety is a prime consideration in the design of any firearm, and sporting guns have been fitted with a variety of safety catches intended to prevent accidental discharge. Early guns had dogs or hooked catches which locked the flintlock cock in a safe position. Later flintlock and percussion guns had a variety of catches, the most common being a sliding bolt fitted to the outside of the lockplate and pushed forward to engage with a recess cut into the cock or hammer to lock it. Joe Manton developed a safety guard which used a bar mounted below the stock; when pressed by the hand it released a small hook which had engaged and locked the trigger. A similar bar safety, developed by Silver, could not be operated until a sliding catch, set at the top of the action, was pushed forward. The same maker also had a 'Silver' stud device mounted on the side of the tumbler which was blocked by an arm on the trigger and was only freed when the trigger was pressed. Greener developed a butt safety bolt which consisted of a rod which passed through the stock and locked the trigger plate. The other end was fitted to a small pivoting block which projected slightly from the back of the butt. When the gun was put to the shoulder, the arm was pressed forward and the pivoted action disengaged the rod from the trigger plate. The majority of safety catches on modern guns are set on the top of the stock, but a few, such as some Greener guns, have a side-mounted catch – some guns have some form of push stud which locks the trigger.

At the end of the nineteenth century, double-barrelled sporting guns were being offered with a single trigger to operate both locks in turn. The idea was not a new one – early wheel-lock and flintlock guns were fitted with the same system – but its re-introduction was hailed as an innovation. The great majority of double-barrelled guns were made with two triggers, but the single trigger is gaining in popularity particularly among American sportsmen and on over-and-under clay pigeon guns.

Accessories
Prior to the development of the pinfire cartridge, most sportsmen on a day's shoot carried powder flask and shot flask. Powder horns and flasks have been in use since the sixteenth century, and until the eighteenth century the majority were fashioned from sections of cowhorn or antler. From the second half of the eighteenth century, however, they were more commonly of copper and from the nineteenth century the variety of design was enormous. Many were embossed with patterns, hunting scenes and motifs, the majority being supplied by two firms, Dixon's and Hawksley's. Some were divided into two or three compartments to hold spare flints or nipples and bullets in addition to the powder.

Shot was carried in leather shot flasks usually fitted with adjustable chargers which could be set to throw a designated charge. An alternative to the flask was the shot belt, which had a leather tube fitted with a charger and was carried slung across the shoulder. Pre-measured charges of shot were carried in double-ended metal containers.

With the introduction of percussion caps the shooter acquired cap dispensers, spring-loaded containers which delivered caps, one at a time, in a device which enabled them to be placed directly onto the nipple.

Cartridges removed the necessity for flasks and shot containers, but introduced reloading gear. In the interests of economy, or because of supply problems, shooters often reloaded the fired cartridge cases. This involved re-sizing the case, replacing the used primer by a fresh one, filling the case with powder and shot and closing the end. A variety of hand and bench tools were designed for these tasks. Quantities of cartridges for organised shoots were carried in magazines which were usually of wood and divided into sections. Each section had a strip of material which was pulled to raise the cartridges within that compartment.

From the late eighteenth century it was increasingly common to supply guns in wooden cases complete with various accessories and tools. Many sporting guns were cased with separate compartments for barrels, stock, oil bottles, cleaning rods and sundry other extras. Most cases had a maker's label stuck on the inside of the lid and a few were supplied with an outer leather carrying case. Some carrying cases were more simple, with compartments only for barrel and stock, and this gave them the characteristic shape known as 'leg-o-mutton'.

For organised shooting-parties it was usual to pick for the various positions in the line and for this purpose a variety of place markers were available. Many consisted of small, numbered ivory rods or plaques which were pulled from a block or other holder. A few were elaborate, the holder being in the form of a cartridge case which opened to display a fan of thin ivory slips. For the very heavy 'bags' at these shoots there were game counters – numbered discs which could be rotated to show the total figures in a 'window'.

In addition to these standard items there was, as with all sports and indeed all human activity, a whole range of gadgets and brilliant ideas which never quite succeeded. Many are hard to identify other than by careful scrutiny of gunmakers' catalogues of the late nineteenth and early twentieth centuries.

Sporting Rifles
In Europe during the eighteenth and nineteenth centuries there was an emphasis on the shooting of game birds, but in other continents such as Africa, Asia and America, there was as much, if not more, emphasis on hunting larger animals. Since the killing power and range of shot is limited, there was a need of a gun to deliver a more powerful missile and give a greater range. The firearm for this was the rifle which, with its grooved barrel, could spin the projectile to

give greater accuracy at longer ranges. There were wheel-lock and flintlock rifles, but the technical problems involved in cutting the spiral grooves on the inside surface of the barrel were formidable, and it was not until the nineteenth century when there were great technical advances that rifles became common. For game shooting a variety of single and double rifles were made by most of the famous London gunmakers. For big game such as elephant and rhino more powerful cartridges were developed, and firms such as Holland & Holland acquired a reputation for powerful 'express' rifles. For a long period, India and Africa were regarded as large game parks where army officers and hunters slaughtered vast numbers of tiger, lion, elephant, hippo and a myriad of other animals. India, in particular, was popular and the Maharajahs and other princes were keen shots and purchased large quantities of sporting guns and rifles from British gunmakers and, to a degree, were responsible for stimulating and maintaining the British gun trade. In the USA rifles had long been more common and from the eighteenth century the famous Kentucky, or more properly, the Pennsylvanian long rifle, had acquired a reputation for accuracy.

Collecting
Apart from the legal aspects discussed elsewhere, the collecting of sporting guns, especially nineteenth-century examples, is one of opportunity, offering the chance of building a comprehensive collection at reasonable cost. The range of both percussion and cartridge actions, barrel designs, stock shapes, safety bolts, cartridges and associated items is enormous and at the time of writing (1983) these items are still readily available at prices within the range of most collectors. It must be emphasised that most of the examples will often be in poor condition and should not be fired under any circumstances. Prior to the invention of smokeless powders all barrels were made to withstand the pressure generated by black powder only, which in general was less than that created by modern 'nitro' powders. It follows that older barrels may well be incapable of withstanding pressures generated by modern powders and the additional factors of age, rust and unseen dents and weaknesses can mean that there is a considerable risk of a burst barrel.

Rust is generally the greatest enemy of all old metal and its action can be stopped by one of the modern preparations such as WD 40 oil or a patent rust remover. Care must be exercised because the action of some of these preparations can be rather vigorous and may etch the metal. This etching property can be used, with great care, to enhance the appearance of Damascus barrels for the steel and iron react in different degrees.

Unless the surface is deeply pitted it may be worth attempting to re-brown earlier barrels, but this requires a good deal of preparation. The surface must be thoroughly cleaned, rust removed and pits smoothed, and the barrel must then be cleansed of all grease. Using one of the browning mixtures, the barrel is then treated and cleaned several times until the required degree of colour is achieved. There are a number of modern mixtures, but in general the original formulae given in such books as W. W. Greener's *The Gun and its Development*, 9th Edition, London 1910, are best, although there may be some difficulty in getting them made up.

Woodwork needs to be thoroughly cleaned, preferably by washing carefully with warm water and then treating with linseed oil or a proprietary wax.

If the gun is to be stripped, it is imperative that screwdrivers of the correct size be used because much minor, but irritating, damage can be caused by using a screwdriver which is inappropriate to the screw head. The blade can slip and scratch metal or wood, or it can burr and chew up the head of the screw.

ACKNOWLEDGMENTS

My sincere thanks to David Winks of Holland & Holland who placed his extensive knowledge of guns and gunmaking at my disposal, read the manuscript and checked the captions. His expertise is invaluable. Thanks are due to Jim Booth of Sothebys' Modern Sporting Guns Department, who also read the manuscript, and to Chris Brunker of Christies for his help with photographs. Unless otherwise indicated all the photographs are by courtesy of Sothebys.

F.W.

SPORTING GUNS

During the past year since the last edition of this volume was published two events have taken place which will affect shooting and consequently prices for some considerable time.

In August the terrible tradegy of the multiple shootings at the small town of Hungerford brought the subject of firearms into sharp focus. The media latched on to an obvious target and made the most of it. Politicians and instant experts, most of whom had little or no understanding of the subject, proposed immediate remedies. The murders were committed with firearms therefore all firearms must be banned! New laws must be introduced at once to stop such a thing happening again. The Home Office promised prompt legislation and some of the suggested solutions mooted were horrendous, being totally impractical and usually unworkable. Shooting organisations reacted slowly, and in some disarray, but eventually recognised the threat to their sport and began to organise, although there was a regrettable tendency for those least in danger to adopt "it's your problem not mine" attitude to other shooting disciplines.

Eventually the Home Office published its proposals and, although some of the more extreme proposals were not included, many of those retained were still awesome. Shotgun ownership was to be made much more restrictive and the *right* of an applicant to possess a shotgun, subject to certain safeguards, was to be removed and the power given to chief constables to decide if the applicant had a "good reason" for having a shotgun. Such power could obviously lead to variations of interpretations although it is said that clear guide lines will be issued to the police. In addition ownership of pump action and self loading shotguns was to be very severely restricted. All this was proposed, with other restrictions, as the result of one tragic action – the first in the twenty years of the 1968 Firearm Act – and in face of declarations from the authorities that they realised this would not affect the criminal acquisition of firearms.

Fortunately Parliament and the Standing Committee took a more realistic approach to the suggested legislation and at the time of writing (February 1988) numerous amendments are being discussed but the final outcome is uncertain. If the proposed restrictions come into force obviously the market will be affected.

The other important event was the dramatic change in the fortunes of the stocks and share markets later in the year. The considerable losses were said to indicate that money would no longer be available for the purchase of leisure items such as antiques and sporting material. Dramatic fall in demand was prophesied and the sale rooms prepared for the worst.

As far as the antique market was involved the first indications of the probable effect were given by a Sotheby sale of antique firearms in Monaco in December 1987. The estimated income was expected to be one million pounds but the final figure was around one million six hundred thousand. Competition was keen and buyers from America and Europe pushed the figures beyond most experts' expectation. It must be pointed out that the items were all of top quality and the upward trend in prices has not been as great for the middle and lower range items. Dealers have found that there is less demand and consequently price rises have not been as steep as in previous years.

Modern sporting guns also showed little sign of a falling demand with buyers from the United States and Europe competing for top quality pieces despite the falling rate of exchange of the dollar. In very general terms modern guns purchased for retail and use by sportsman have shown about a ten percent rise in prices. There have been notable exceptions and a few cases where there was a rise of twenty percent from August to December for equivalent quality guns. There was one very surprising occasion when a Royal pair of Purdey guns built some years ago realised more than the retail price of a new pair. As usual any personal association with people of note pushed up prices in both the antique and the modern and vintage markets.

At the moment all that can be said with any certainty is that the markets are fairly robust although less so than in previous years but what the effects of the present difficulties will be are impossible to predict.

PRICE GUIDE

The prices shown are intended as a broad guide only; there are so many variables where condition of the gun is concerned, but they do indicate what one might expect to pay in auctions for these pieces. If buying from a dealer, his quoted price is likely to be higher in order to allow for a profit margin. The higher-priced items are included more to indicate the range of prices than for collecting purposes.

1. £3000–£3500	**66.** £800–£1200	**130.** £1500–£2000
2. £1800–£2000	**67.** £4000–£6000	**131.** £400–£500
3. £3000–£3500	**68.** £3000–£4000	**132, 133, 134.** £600–£1200
4. £2000–£3000	**69.** £3000–£4000	**136.** £2500–£3500
5. 6. £1500–£2000	**70.** £4000–£5000	**137.** £1000–£1500
7. £4000–£6000	**71.** £4000–£6000	**138.** £1200–£1500
11-14. £500–£800	**72.** £900–£1200	**139.** £800–£900
15. £2000–£2200	**73.** £900–£1200	**140.** £500–£700
16. £3000–£3500	**74.** £700–£1000	**141.** £1400–£1600
17. £2500–£3000	**75.** £2500–£3500	**142.** £1000–£1500
18. £3000–£4000	**76.** £900–£1200	**143.** £700–£900
19. £1000–£1500	**77.** £1200–£1400	**144.** £1000–£1500
20. £2000–£2500	**78.** £500–£600	**145.** £350–£500
21. £2500–£3000	**79.** £2000–£2200	**146.** £1200–£1600
22. £10,000–£12,000	**80.** £1000–£1500	**147.** £2000–£2500
23. £1500–£2000	**81.** £1500–£2000	**148.** £300–£400
24. £2500–£3000	**82.** £1200–£1800	**149.** £400–£500
25. £15,000–£16,000	**83.** £500–£800	**150.** £400–£600
26. £10,000–£12,000	**84.** £5000–£7000	**151.** £300–£400
27. £1400–£1600	**85.** £1000–£1500	**152.** £400–£600
28. £2000–£3000	**86.** £900–£1200	**153, 154.** £400–£600
29. £2000–£3000	**87.** £2000–£3000	**155.** £3500–£4500
30. £3000–£4000	**88.** £1200–£1800	**156.** £3500–£4000
31. £1500–£2000	**89.** £750–£900	**157.** £3000–£4000
32. £1200–£1500	**90.** £800–£1200	**158.** £5500–£7000
33. £1200–£1500	**93, 94.** £4000–£6000	**159.** £2500–£3500
34. £1500–£1800	**95.** £1000–£1500	**160.** £4000–£5000 (pair)
35. £2000–£3000	**96.** £1500–£2500 (pair)	**161.** £2500–£3000
36. £2000–£2600	**97.** £500–£700	**162.** £2000–£3000
37. £1200–£1800	**98.** £1500–£2000	**163.** £1500–£2000
38. £1000–£1200	**99.** £1000–£1500	**164.** £400–£500
39. £3000–£5000	**100.** £400–£600	**165.** £700–£900
40. £2500–£3500	**101.** £1000–£1500	**166.** £1500–£2000
41. £800–£1000	**102.** £1000–£1500	**167.** £500–£800
42. £700–£900	**104, 105.** £300–£400	**168.** £600–£800
43. £800–£1000	**106.** £600–£800	**169.** £7000–£9000 (pair)
44. £800–£1000	**107, 108.** £2000–£3000	**170.** £800–£900
45. £800–£1000	**109.** £600–£700	**172.** £4000–£5000 (pair)
46. £700–£900	**110.** £500–£600	**173.** £4000–£5000
47. £400–£600*	**111.** £300–£400	**175.** £1400–£1800
48. £300–£500*	**112..** £5000–£6000	**176.** £140–£160
49, 50. £3000–£4000	**113.** £800–£1000	**177.** £200–£250
51. £500–£700	**114.** £600–£800	**178.** £40–£60
52. £800–£1000*	**115.** £600–£900	**179.** £25–£300
53. £2500–£3000	**116.** £800–£1200	**180.** £400–£450
54. £2500–£3000	**117.** £600–£900	**181.** £600–£700
55. £4000–£6000	**118.** £800–£1000	**182.** £700–£900
56, 57. £3000–£4000	**119, 120.** £2000–£3000	**183.** £400–£600
58. £900–£1200	**121.** £900–£1200	**184.** £400–£500
59. £500–£700	**122.** £600–£800	**187.** reloading £300–£350 clay pigeon thrower £50–£80
60. £500–£600	**123.** £1000–£1200	**188.** reloading £300–£350 duck £60–£100
61. £700–£900	**124.** £300–£400	**189.** £150–£300
62. £7000–£9000	**125, 126.** £500–£700	**190, 191.** £30,000–£35,000
63. £700–£900	**127.** £150–£200	**192, 193.** £2500–£5000
64. £1200–£1400	**128.** £600–£800	
65. £1500–£2000	**129.** £1200–£1400	

*Composite pieces such as these guns obviously realise lower prices than those with all original parts.

THE LAW AND COLLECTING

In Britain the 1968 Firearms Act governs all matters concerning firearms and in some respects its provisions can give rise to problems. Antique firearms can be collected without any restrictions provided they are kept as 'curiosities or ornaments'. If the collector wishes to fire them they no longer count as antiques and some form of legal permission is required to hold them. 'Antique' is generally taken to cover all types of firearms up to and including percussion-cap weapons, but the situation then becomes confused. Some police authorities will accept pinfire weapons and some of the very early cartridge weapons as antiques, other authorities refuse to consider any of these as antiques. Since 1977, and the case of Curwen v Richards, it has been held that any case concerned with the definition of 'antique' must be decided by a magistrate and this can lead to some very strange anomalies.

Non-antique, smooth-bore sporting guns can be held on a Shotgun Certificate provided that the barrels exceed 24 inches in length, and at the time of writing (August 1983) there is no restriction on the number of weapons held on one certificate. In order to acquire a Shotgun Certificate, however, police approval is required and the local Crime Prevention Officer may impose certain security requirements on the collector which must be met before a certificate will be granted. It is to be hoped that the officer will appreciate that old shotguns present very little security risk.

Rifled weapons and smooth-bore weapons having a barrel less than 24 inches in length can only be held on a Firearm Certificate which is much more difficult to obtain. The police are likely to be far more insistent on high security before granting a Firearm Certificate. Even if one is granted it gives authority only to hold certain specified weapons, and each change of weapon means a fresh application for a variation. It was once possible to obtain a Firearm Certificate for collecting purposes, but unhappily few police authorities are prepared to grant such certificates now. It may be possible to obtain a Registered Firearms Dealer Certificate which allows its owner to acquire and dispose of weapons without having to apply for a variation to a Firearm Certificate each time. Before the granting of a Registered Firearms Dealer Certificate the police are certain to insist on a very high standard of security and, if granted, all conditions relative to a dealer must be observed.

BIBLIOGRAPHY

ACTION, J. *An Essay on Shooting.* London, 1791

AKEHURST, R. *Game Guns and Rifles.* London, 1969

— *Sporting Guns.* London, 1969

ARNOLD, R. *Automatic & Repeating Shotguns.* London, 1976

BAILEY D. W., & NIE, D. *English Gunmakers.* London, 1978

BEARSE, R. *Sporting Arms of the World.* London, 1976

BLACKMORE, H. *Guns and Rifles of the World.* London, 1965

— *Hunting Weapons.* London, 1971

— *Royal Sporting Guns at Windsor.* London, 1968

BLANCH, H. J. *A Century of Guns.* London, 1909

BRANDER, M. *Hunting and Shooting.* London, 1971

BURRARD, G. *The Modern Shotgun*, 3 Vols. London, 1931–48

CRUDINGTON, I., & BAKER, D. J. *The British Shotgun*, Vol. I 1850–70. London, 1979

DAEHNHARDT, R. *Espingarda Perfeyta.* Reprint London, 1974

DANIEL, W. B. *Rural Sports.* London, 1801

GLADSTONE, H. S. *Record Bags and Shooting Records.* London, 1930

GOUGH, T. *Shotguns and Cartridges.* London, 1970

GREENER, W. W. *The Gun.* London, 1835

— *The Gun and its Development.* London, 9th edn, 1910

HALLOCK, C. *Sportsman's Gazeteer.* New York, 1880

HANGER, G. *To all Sportsmen.* London, 1814

HARRIS, C. (ed.) *The History of the Birmingham Gun-Barrel Proof House.* Birmingham, 1946

HARRISON, E. *Dissertation on Guns.* London, 1906

HASTINGS, M. *English Sporting Guns and Accessories.* London, 1969

— *The Shotgun.* London, 1981

HAWKER, Lieutenant-Colonel P. *Instructions to Young Sportsmen in all that relates to Guns and Shooting.* London, 1814

JOHNSTON, T. B. *The Shooter's Preceptor.* London, 1844

LANCASTER, C. *The Art of Shooting.* London, 1938

LEWIS, J. *Shotgun Digest.* Northfield, 1980

'MARKSMAN' *The Dead Shot.* London, 1960

MILLS, J. *Sportsman's Library.* London, 1845

NEAL, W. K. & BACK, D. H. *Forsyth & Co., Patent Gunmakers.* London, 1969

— *British Gunmakers*: their Trade Cards, Cases and Equipment, 1760–1860. Warminster, 1980

OLSON, J. *The Shotgun.* New Jersey, 1975

PURDEY, T. D., & J. A. *The Shotgun.* London, 1977

RILING, R. *The Powder Flask Book.* New Hope, Penn., 1953

SANDYS-WINCH, G. *Gun Law.* London, 1979

TEASDALE-BUCKELL, G. T. *Experts on Guns and Shooting.* London, 1900

THOMAS, B. *The Shooter's Guide.* London, 1816

WALSH, J. H. *The Modern Sportsman's Gun and Rifle*, Vol. I London, 1882; Vol. II London, 1884

WATERMAN, C. *Treasury of Sporting Guns.* London, 1979

WATT, W. *Remarks on Shooting.* London, 1835

WEBBER, A. *Shooting.* London, 1841

WIRNSBERGER, G. *The Standard Directory of Proof Marks.* New Jersey, 1975

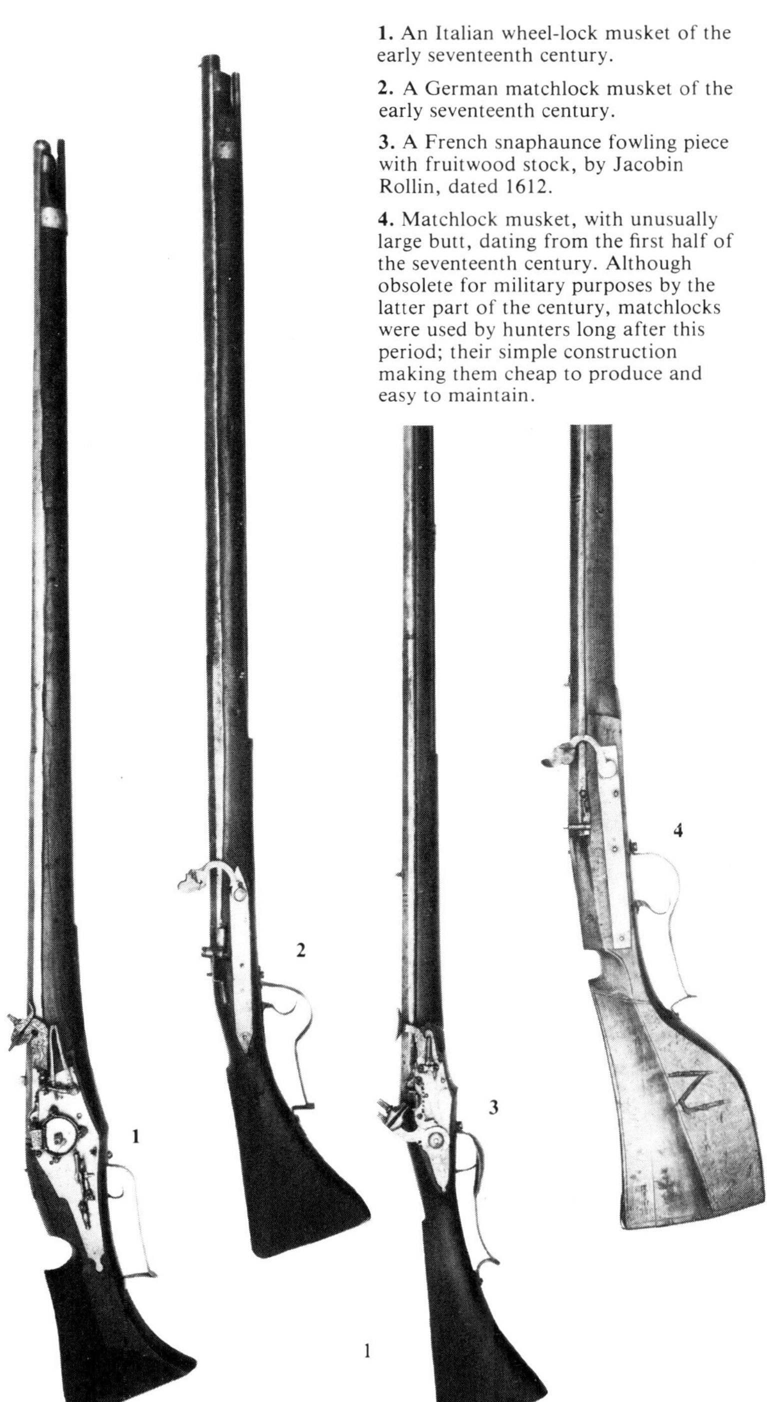

1. An Italian wheel-lock musket of the early seventeenth century.

2. A German matchlock musket of the early seventeenth century.

3. A French snaphaunce fowling piece with fruitwood stock, by Jacobin Rollin, dated 1612.

4. Matchlock musket, with unusually large butt, dating from the first half of the seventeenth century. Although obsolete for military purposes by the latter part of the century, matchlocks were used by hunters long after this period; their simple construction making them cheap to produce and easy to maintain.

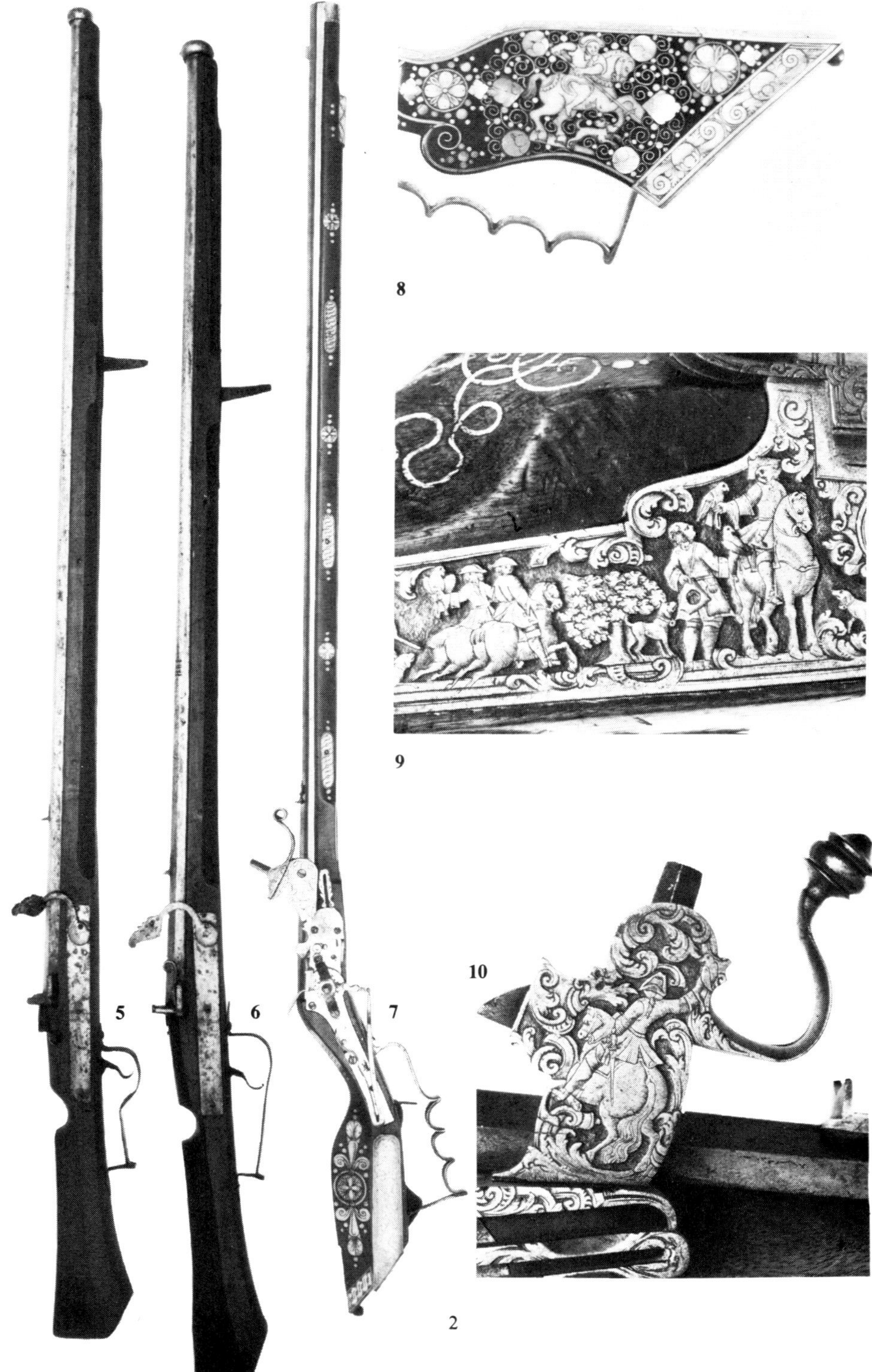

5 and 6. Beneath the stock of these wall guns are projecting lugs which were hooked over a parapet or wall to absorb the recoil and steady the aim. Both these matchlocks date from the early seventeenth century, and the top one bears the SUHL town mark.

7. A typical light, birding Tschinke wheel-lock rifle, with its characteristic strongly curved butt, inlaid decoration and external lock. A recess with sliding lid in the butt housed patches for the bullets. As on most wheel-locks the trigger guard is contoured for the fingers.

8. This mounted huntsman and his dog are part of the inlaid decoration on the butt of a Tschinke. The metal ball at the tip of the butt protected the decoration when the gun was stood on its butt.

9 and 10. The superb craftsmanship of the gunmaker is clearly visible in these enlarged photographs of the chiselling on a wheel-lock gun of the seventeenth century.

11. A Bohemian wheel-lock made by Mathias Kurtzweil of Prague about 1700.

12. South German wheel-lock of the early seventeenth century.

13. South German wheel-lock of the late seventeenth century.

14. German wheel-lock of the early seventeenth century.

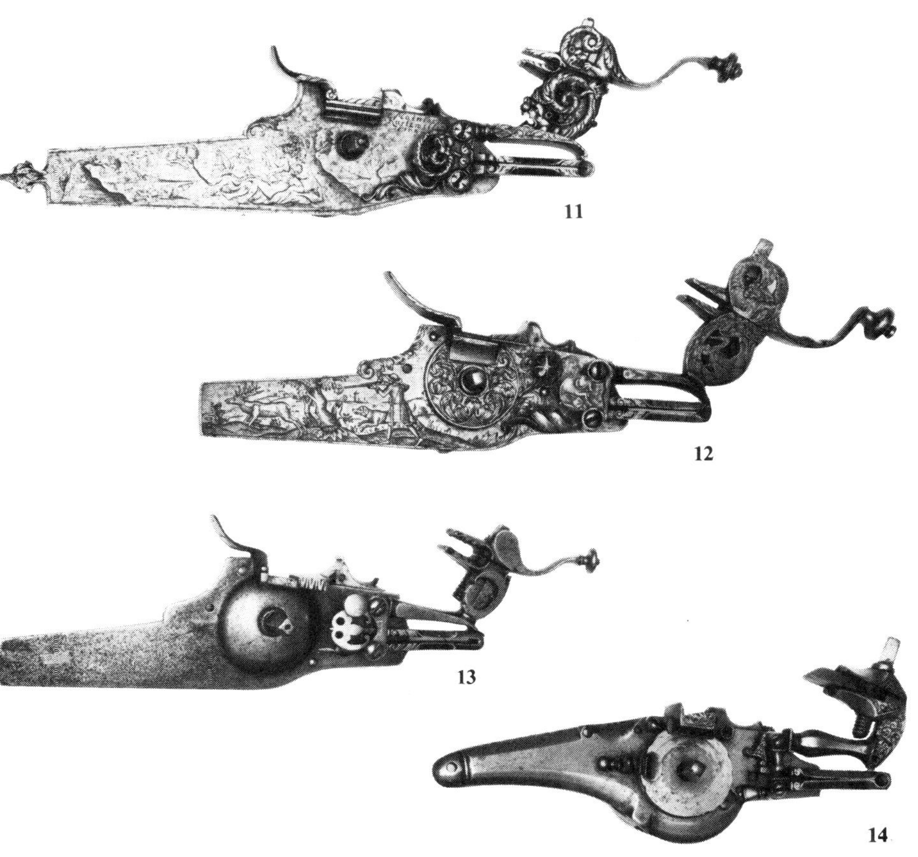

11

12

13

14

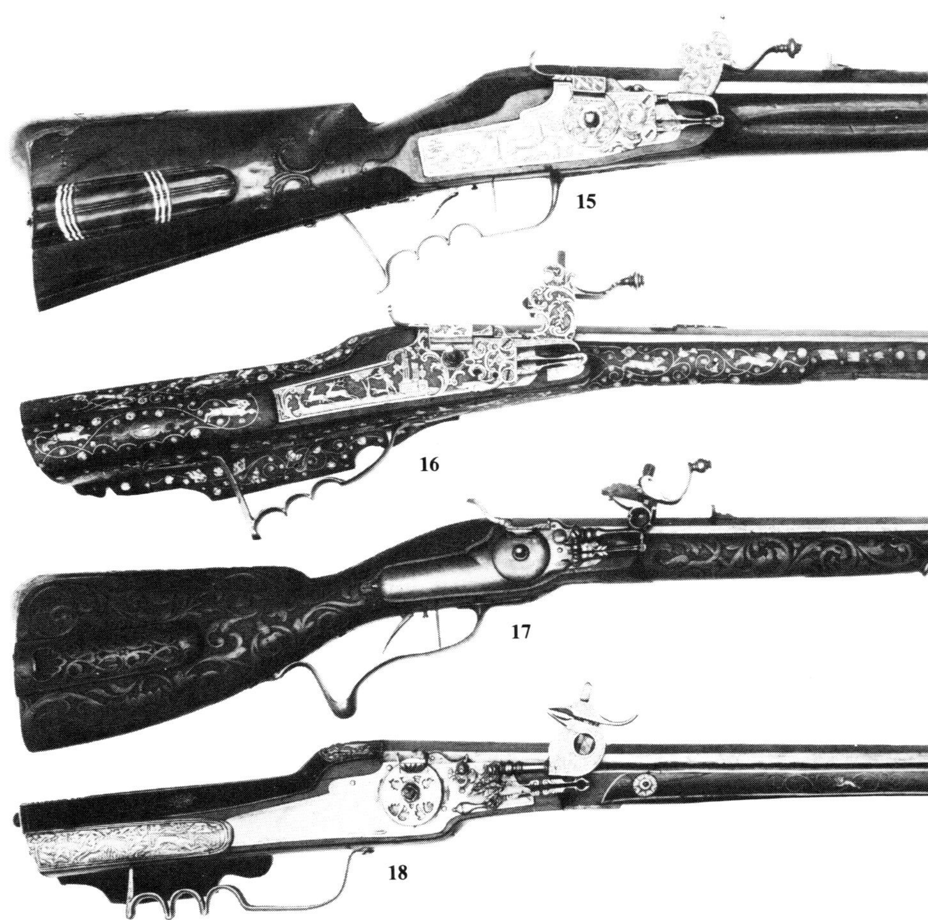

15, 16, 17 and 18. Sporting Wheel-lock Rifles. **15.** Barrel with nine grooves; signed on the breech JOHANN FRIDRICH LIMMER IN BAMBERG; the lock is signed H.W.EINIG. Dating from the mid seventeenth century. **16.** A decorative German rifle dating from the mid seventeenth century; the lock is signed JOHANN ENGST. **17.** German sporting rifle of the late seventeenth century. **18.** The butt shape indicates that this Saxon rifle was made early in the seventeenth century. (Note that two of these rifles have hair-triggers, a common feature on good quality weapons.)

19. Composite wheel-lock target rifle, ten-groove rifling, breech signed MARTIN SUSSELBECKER IN DRESDEN FECIT 1649; hair-trigger, brass furniture, restocked in the mid eighteenth century.

20. German wheel-lock sporting rifle, eight-groove rifling, plain lock, early seventeenth century.

21. German sporting rifle with seven-groove rifling, the wheel enclosed by pierced brass sheet; walnut stock, hair-trigger, early eighteenth century.

22. Superimposed load wheel-lock sporting rifle, the barrel dated 1593 and bearing maker's mark ZACHARIAS HEROLD, eight-groove rifling, the lock marked CHRISTOF DRESSLER, full stock with animals and fabulous beasts inlaid in bone. Late sixteenth century. This rifle has two locks for the two charges loaded into the breech and discharged one at a time.

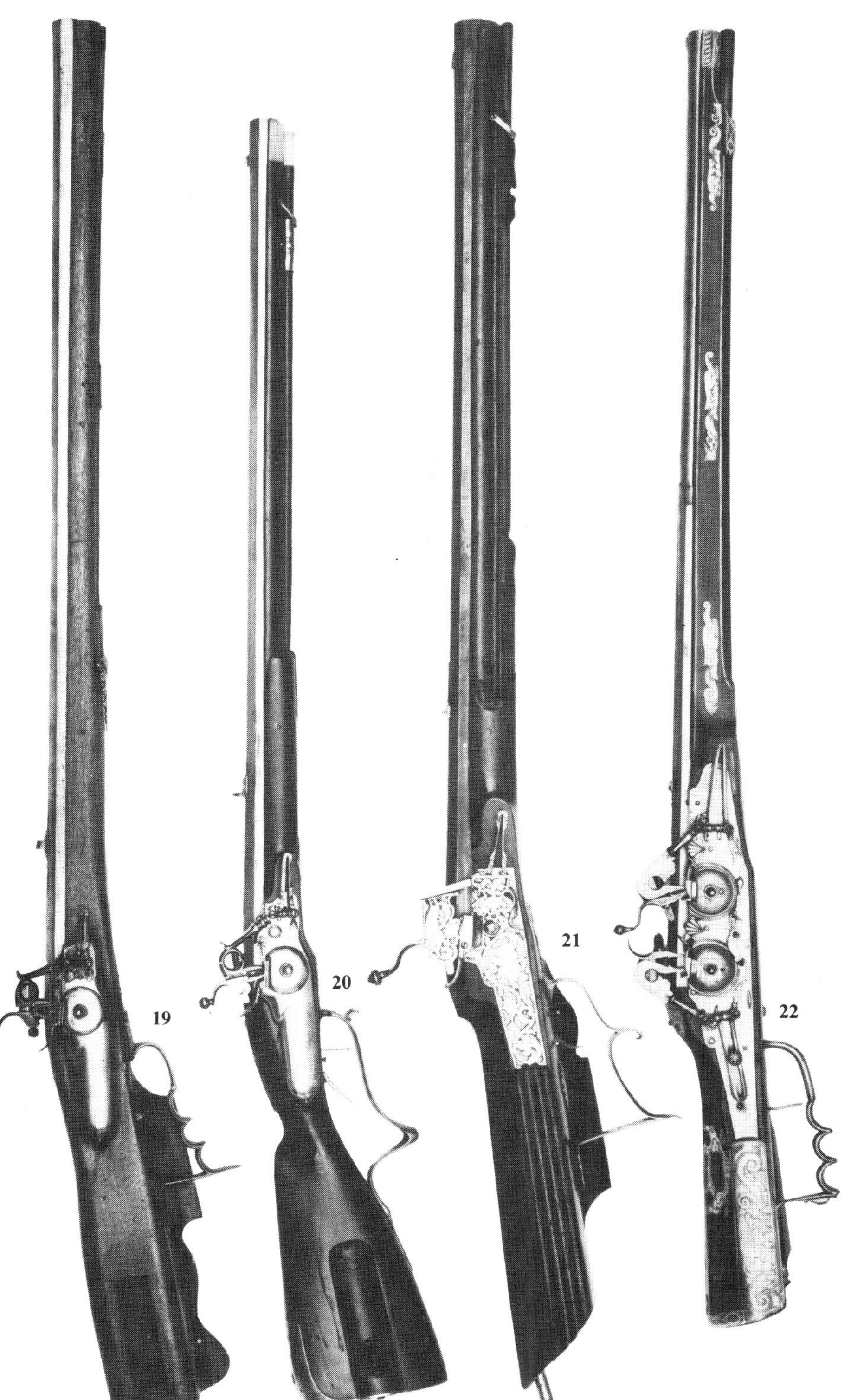

19
20
21
22

23. A central Italian snaphaunce musket, the lock plate engraved with foliate scrolls. The fruitwood stock is similar to that found on wheel-lock guns of the same period – mid seventeenth century.

24. Decorative German hunting rifle, the barrel having nine-groove rifling and bearing the initials VB. The lock is engraved and has a dog-catch – the hook which engages with a notch at the back of the cock – a feature that was largely abandoned early in the eighteenth century although it was re-introduced on some later weapons. The full stock of walnut is inlaid with wire. Circa 1700.

25. This Swiss duck gun dating from about 1660 has an octagonal barrel and a snaphaunce lock signed by Jacques Aubert, a gunmaker of Geneva. The large butt is found on many muskets of this period, especially on those from around the Mediterranean.

26. German birding rifle with six-groove rifling, mid seventeenth century. The swan-neck cock is fitted with a dog-catch and the lock has a hair-trigger. The fruitwood stock has a number of inset chiselled plaques of animals and the butt has a larger plaque which portrays an amorous couple.

27. A German flintlock rifle with octagonal, eight-grooved barrel, and an elaborately carved butt and stock. Circa 1700.

28. German flintlock rifle with barrel dated 1729 and bearing the shield of Hans Löffer of Grund (Hanover). It has an unusually large trigger guard.

29. Spanish sporting gun, the barrel bearing the legend FRANCO BIS MADRID ANO 1740 inlaid in gold. The Madrid lock is also signed. Spanish barrels were highly prized and this one was fitted with a new stock later in the eighteenth century.

30. A Dutch flintlock sporting gun with a two-stage barrel; the lock signed by a Maastricht maker, Oger Leblan. The lock and barrel are mounted in a stock with a butt of Spanish form. First half of the eighteenth century.

31. Hungarian flintlock musket fitted with a Turkish barrel inlaid with silver and gold. The chiselled lock is signed IOH FISCHER IN PRESBURG. Bronze furniture adorns the three-quarter stock. Circa 1730–40.

32. Flemish fowling piece with barrel of Spanish form, chiselled lock signed HENOUR, circa 1730.

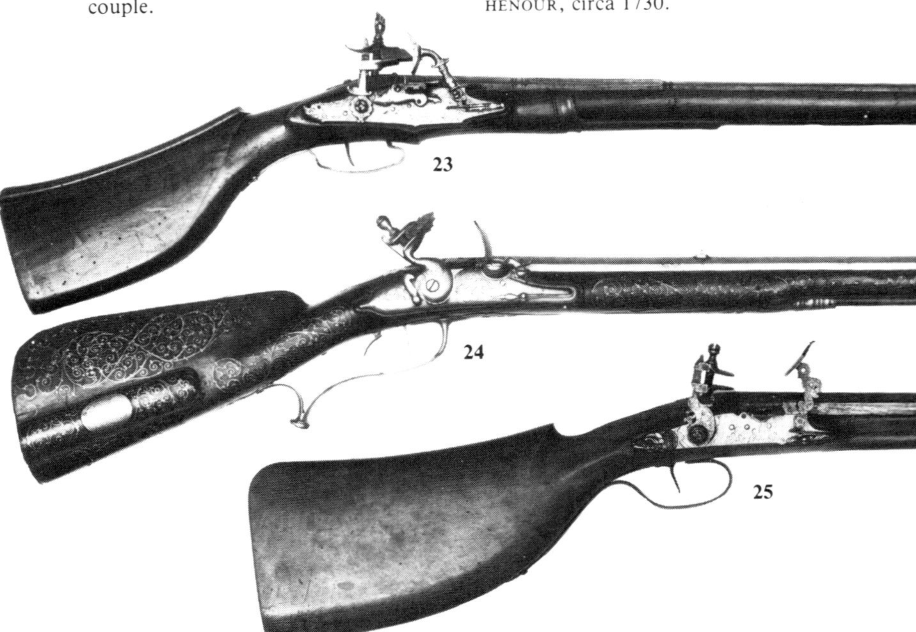

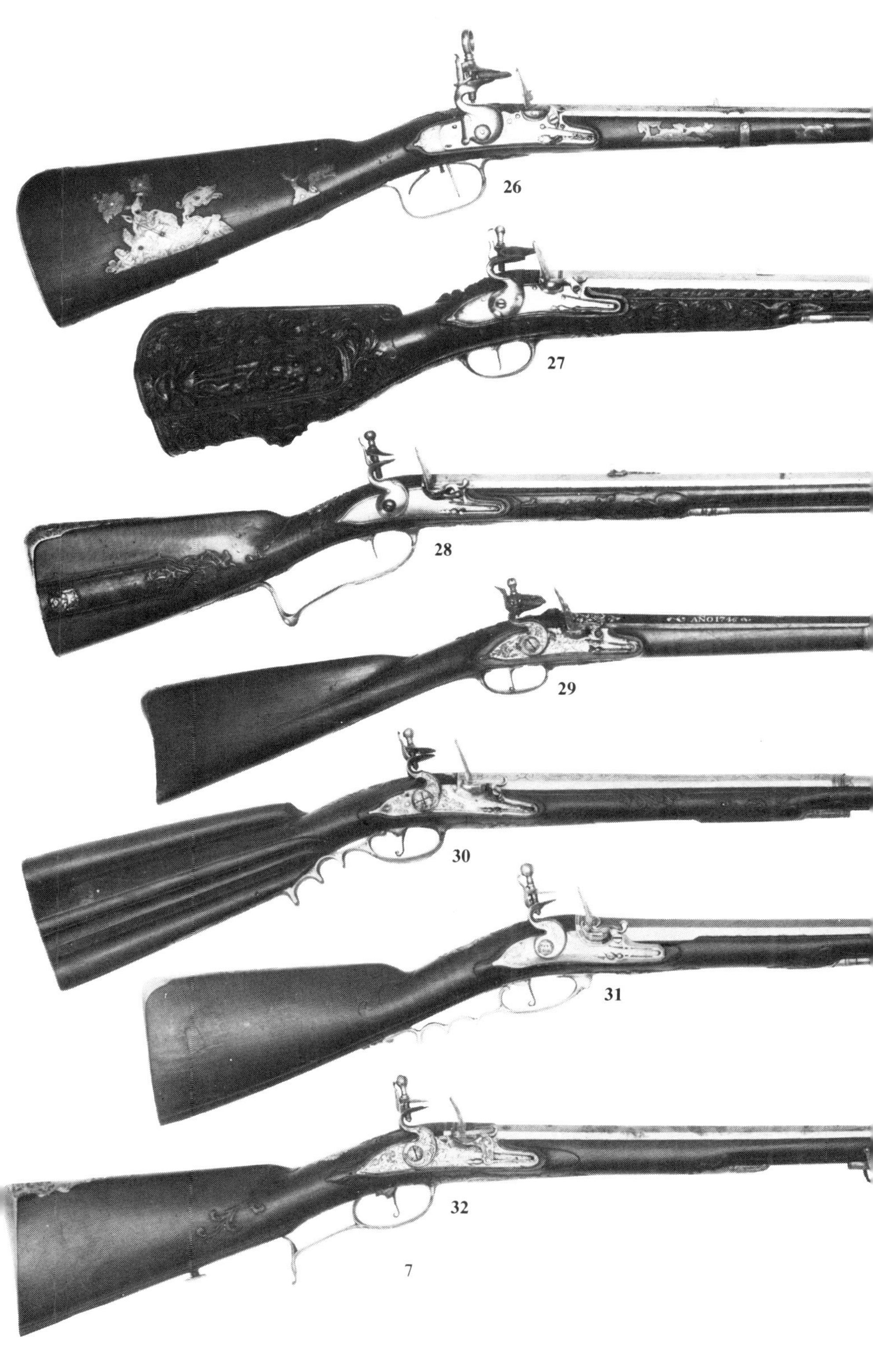
26
27
28
29
30
31
32
7

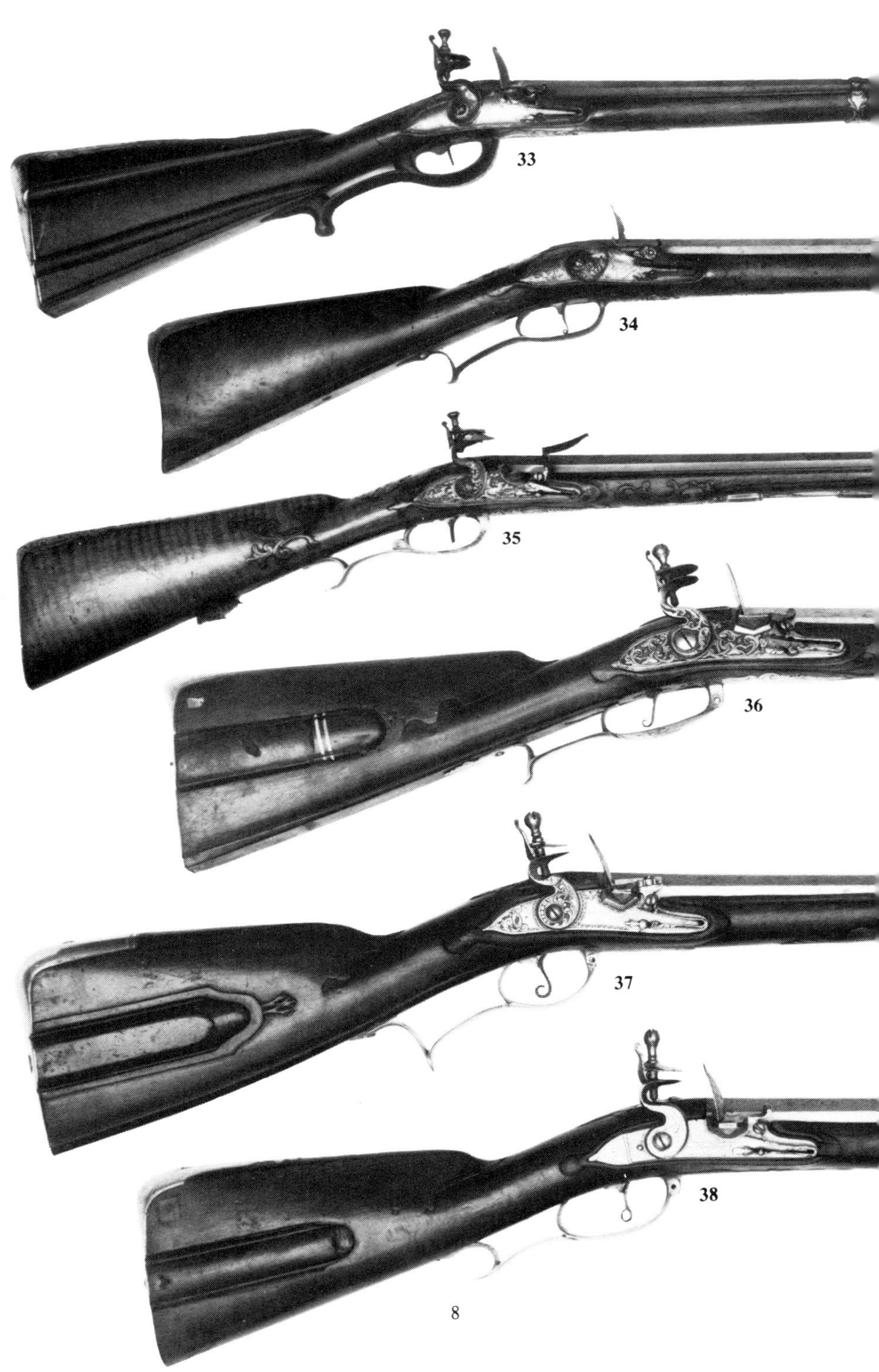

33
34
35
36
37
38

33. German or Austrian sporting
flintlock gun with a blued and gilt
Spanish barrel bearing marks of
Madrid maker Manuel Sutil (1731–41).
As with so many Continental guns the
trigger guard is of wood. Circa 1760.

34. Austrian sporting gun, the barrel
by Simon Penzereter who worked in
about 1720; the stock, however, is
later, about 1750. The lock is chiselled
with figures and trophies – lacking
cock.

35. German gun by Johann Jakob
Kuchenreuter, the lock chiselled with
hunting motif, some carving to the half
stock. Circa 1770.

36. One of a pair of hunting rifles – the
barrel with eight grooves and the
breech bearing the mark of C. Keiner.
The lock and cock are deeply chiselled
with scrolls and the butt has lightly
carved decoration. Circa 1720.

37. Another flintlock hunting rifle with
seven-grooved rifling, numbered '20' on
the tang. The engraved lock has one
interesting feature: as an extra safety
measure the pan cover can be pivoted
laterally clear of the flint. First half of
the eighteenth century.

38. Another rifle of similar date, the
lock signed WOHLFAHRT A POSNECK. As
with most rifles the butts of these three
are fitted with patchboxes.

39. A rare German breech-loading
magazine carbine fitted with the
Lorenzoni action; turn-off octagonal
barrel, seven-groove rifling, brass
frame inscribed FECIT ET INVENIT
WETSCHGI AUGUSTAE, plain brass lock,
swan-neck cock chiselled with dolphin's
head. Loading and cocking lever,
shaped like a serpent, closes the pan
cover and half cocks the action.
Walnut butt with some carving, brass
furniture, hinged cover for loading
with ball and powder. The Lorenzoni
action utilised magazines in the butt to
hold powder and balls which were fed
into the breech by a rotating block.
First quarter of the eighteenth century.

40. Boy's Spanish Miquelet sporting
gun, barrel with gold front sight; EN
MADRID, FRANCISCO TARGARONA ANO DE
1788 and maker's mark engraved on
breech. Gold vent, London proof,
fluted butt, engraved iron furniture.
This maker was one of four designated
as royal gunsmiths by Carlos IV
(1788–1808) on 27 October 1792. Circa
1788.

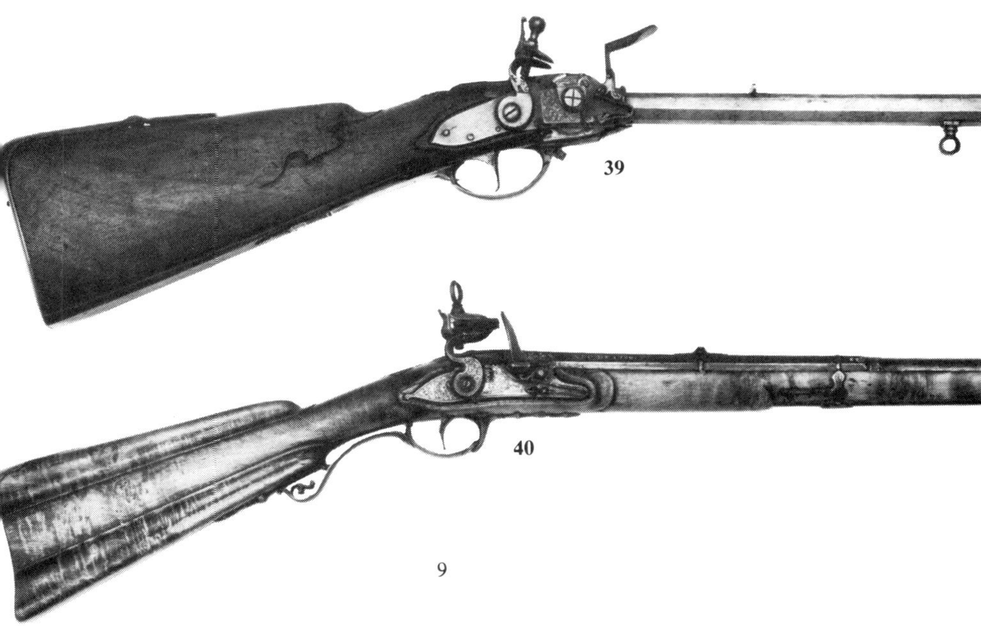

39

40

41
42
43
44
45
46

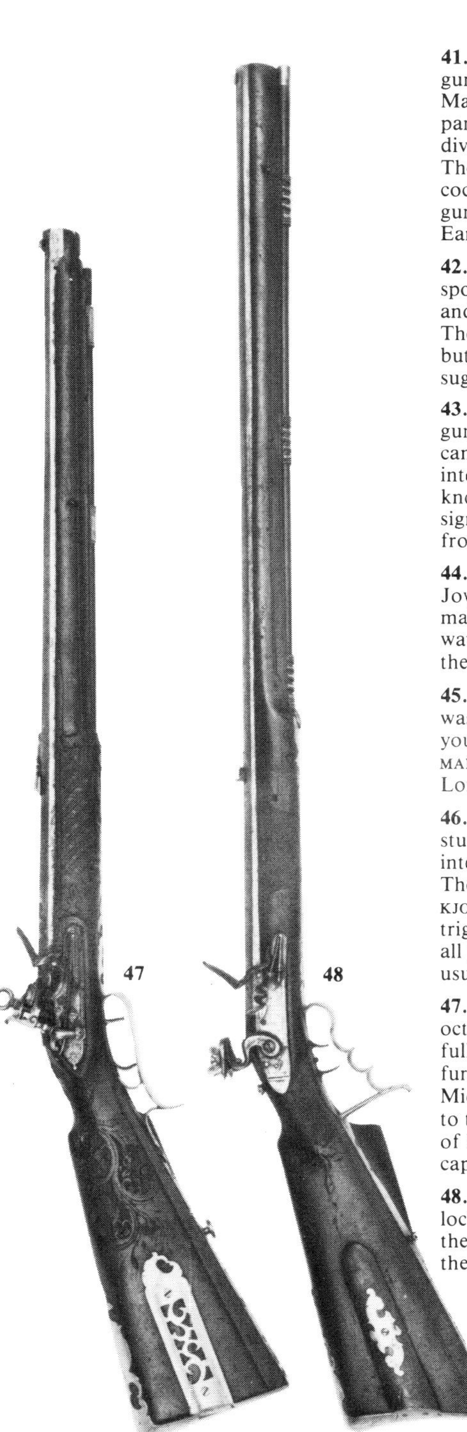

41. French double-barrelled sporting gun, the locks signed by Bizouard of Marseilles. The locks have waterproof pans, so shaped that raindrops were diverted from the priming in the pan. The curling spurs at the top of the cocks are commonly found on French guns, as is the carving on the butt. Early nineteenth century.

42. An unusual double-barrelled sporting gun with one smooth barrel and the other with seven-groove rifling. The signature on the breech is illegible, but the general design of the gun suggests a Flemish maker.

43. Another Flemish double-barrelled gun, but with a single lock; the barrels can be rotated to bring each in turn into the firing position – this system is known as a Wender gun. The lock is signed DE VILLIERS and the gun dates from circa 1770.

44. English flintlock sporting gun by Jover of London – a well known maker; half stocked and fitted with a waterproof pan and a roller bearing on the frizzen spring. Circa 1780.

45. This gun is on a smaller scale and was probably made for a boy or a young man. The lock is signed JOHN MANTON, one of the most famous of London makers. Circa 1785.

46. This Danish flintlock rifle is of very sturdy construction and may have been intended primarily as a target weapon. The lock is signed DELCOMYN KJOBENHAVN and is fitted with a hair-trigger. The stock, butt and barrel are all just a little more substantial than is usual on a hunting rifle. Circa 1800.

47. A German sporting rifle, the octagonal barrel struck M.D IN V. with full stock carved and with brass furniture. The lock is a Spanish Miquelet and did not originally belong to this weapon. The barrel shows signs of having been converted to percussion cap and then re-converted to flint.

48. This weapon also has an associated lock which is signed DAVIDSON although the rifle was made in Bavaria early in the nineteenth century.

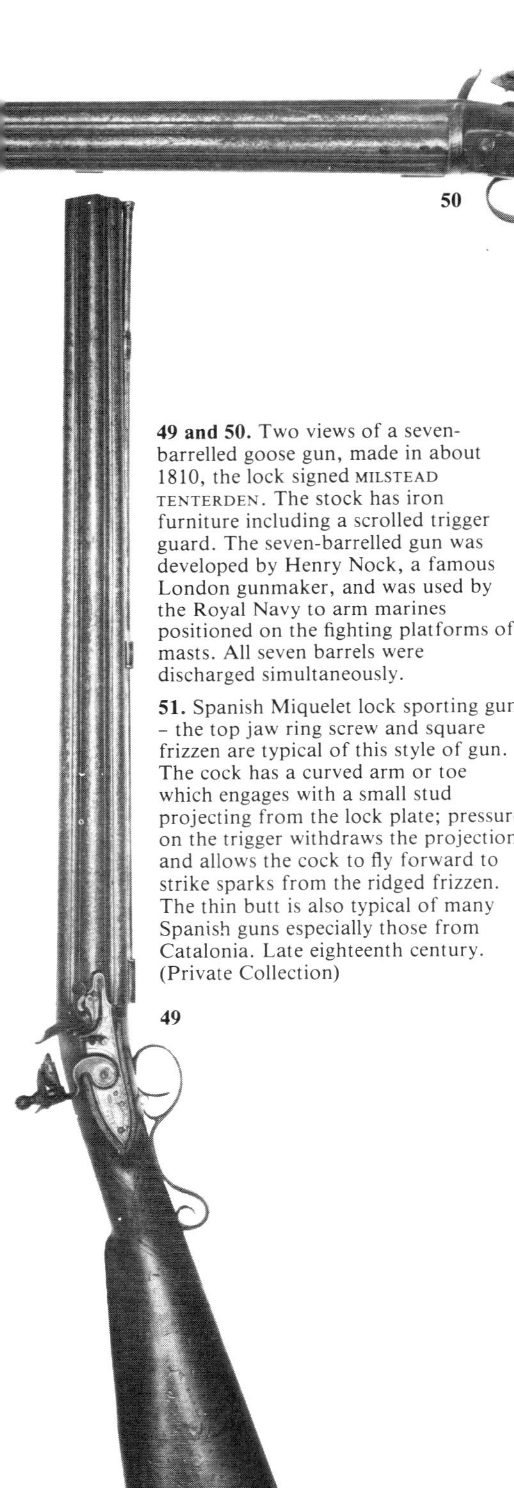

50

49

49 and 50. Two views of a seven-barrelled goose gun, made in about 1810, the lock signed MILSTEAD TENTERDEN. The stock has iron furniture including a scrolled trigger guard. The seven-barrelled gun was developed by Henry Nock, a famous London gunmaker, and was used by the Royal Navy to arm marines positioned on the fighting platforms of masts. All seven barrels were discharged simultaneously.

51. Spanish Miquelet lock sporting gun – the top jaw ring screw and square frizzen are typical of this style of gun. The cock has a curved arm or toe which engages with a small stud projecting from the lock plate; pressure on the trigger withdraws the projection and allows the cock to fly forward to strike sparks from the ridged frizzen. The thin butt is also typical of many Spanish guns especially those from Catalonia. Late eighteenth century. (Private Collection)

52. As is common with many sporting guns this flintlock fowling piece is of mixed origin. The barrel and lock are French, dated 1720 and signed ST. GERMAIN A PARIS, but the stock is German and dates from about the middle of the eighteenth century.

53. One of a pair of Austrian sporting guns, by Joseph Hammel of Vienna, with Spanish-style barrels. The butts are designed for a left-handed man since the cheek rest is on the right side of the butt. The trigger guard is wooden. Mid eighteenth century.

54. One of another pair by Christopher Riss of Vienna, also with Spanish-type barrels and, again, designed to be fired left-handed. Circa 1750.

55. A top quality, French double-barrelled flintlock sporting gun by the master craftsman Nicolas-Noël Boutet whose name appears on the barrel together with his title – DIRECTEUR ARTISTE A VERSAILLE. The barrels carry the mark of the famous maker Nicholas Le Clerc. The cocks and butt are typical of this period in French gunmaking. Circa 1810–15.

56 and 57. German double-barrelled flintlock fowling piece; browned twist barrels with some gold decoration and vents, the locks engraved and one signed F.S. ADLER and the other STETIN; unusual push-on safety catches and waterproof pans, silver furniture. The full stock has fine carved decoration; the dolphin's head pistol grip has inset ivory eyes. The silver trigger guard is decorated with a hunter shooting at a deer and a cartouche depicting a Red Indian. At one time this gun was owned by Field Marshal Sir George Pollock (1786–1872).

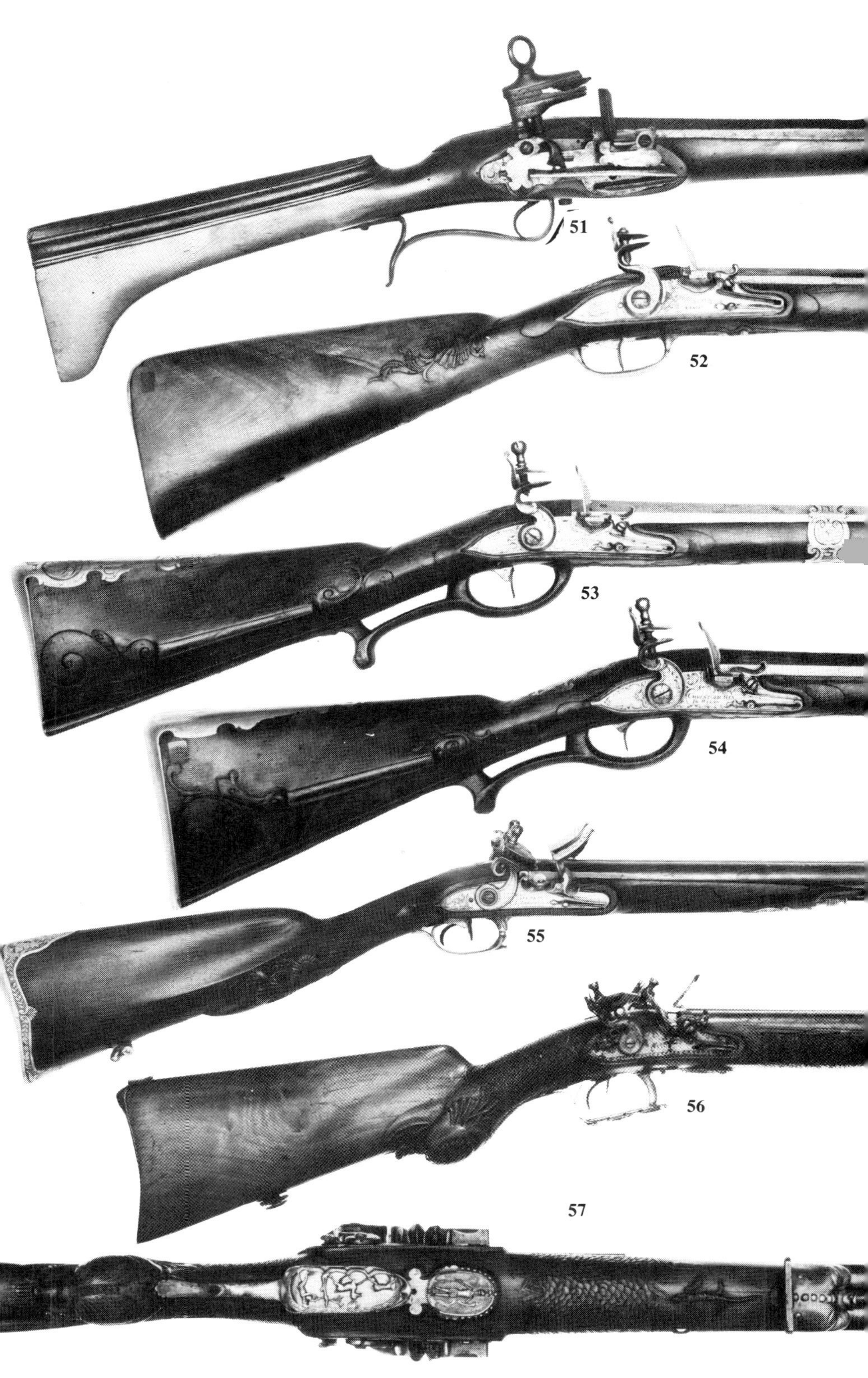

51
52
53
54
55
56
57

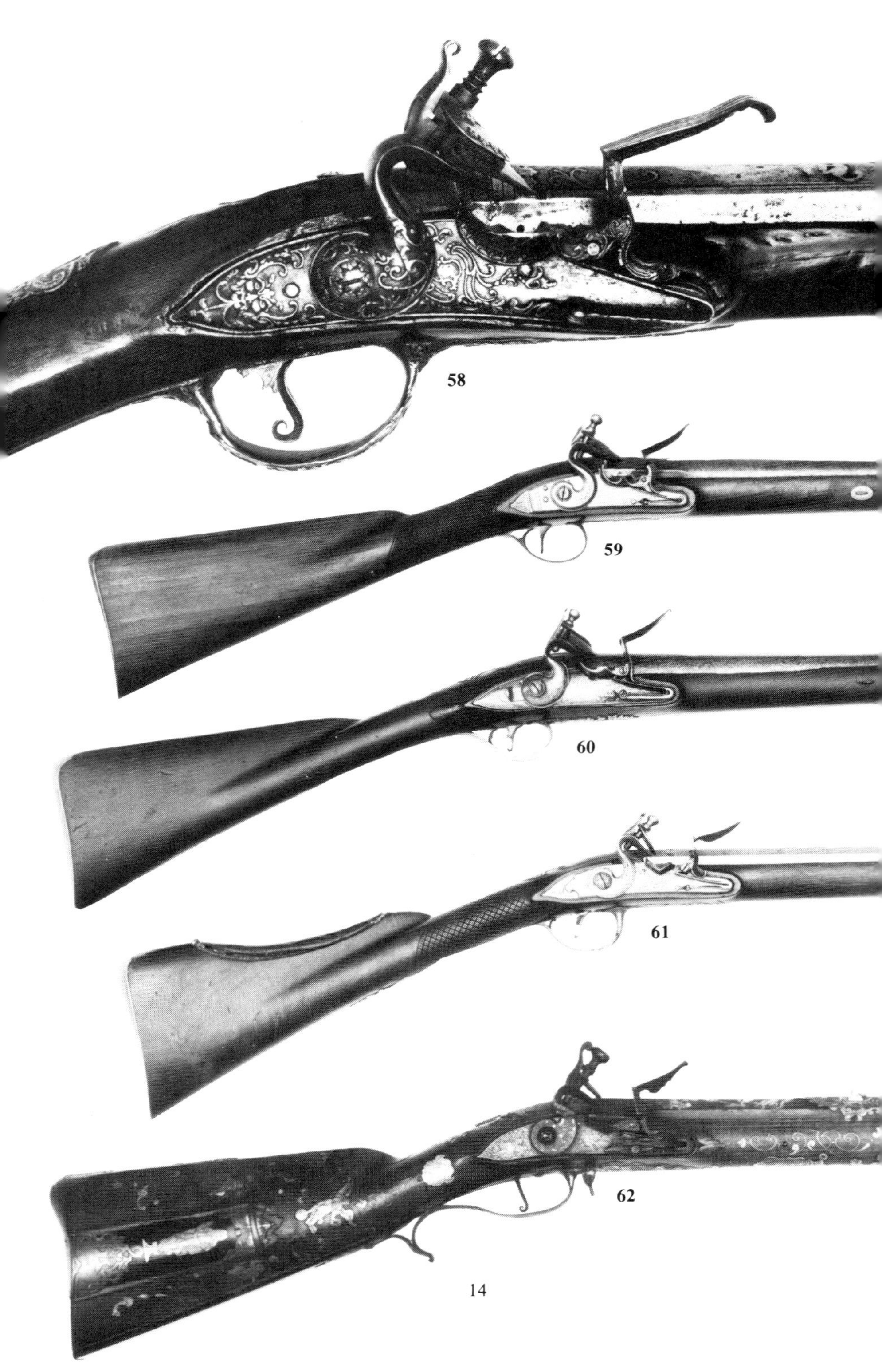

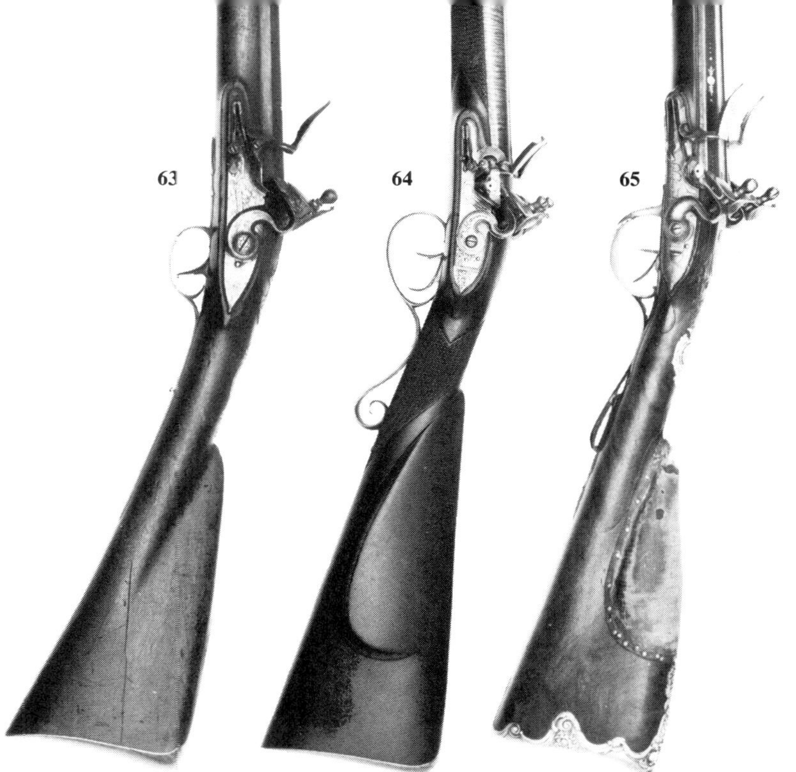

58. Metal workers in the north of Italy around Brescia were noted for their skill and craftsmanship, and the delicate chiselling on this lock is typical of their work. The slight 'banana' shape to the lock and the backward curve at the bottom of the trigger are usually found on guns of the very late seventeenth and early eighteenth centuries. (Private Collection)

59. English flintlock fowling piece with Damascus barrel, gold decoration at the breech and signed H.NOCK; the lock is signed JACKSON. Circa 1780.

60. An earlier English flintlock fowling piece, well made, but without any names or marks. Mid eighteenth century.

61. French flintlock fowling piece with Spanish-style barrel by Le Clerc, the lock signed DE SAINTE A VERSAILLES. The butt has a leather-covered cheek pad. Circa 1780.

62. A German flintlock sporting rifle, the octagonal barrel having seven-groove rifling and inlaid with gold and silver. The lock is signed in gold by JOHANN WAGNER IN CRONACK, who is recorded as having worked in the period 1715–75. Full walnut stock inlaid with silver wire scrolls and plaques; the butt has an ebony butt cap inlaid with an armoured man. Circa 1720–30.

63. This sporting gun was specially made for a left-handed shooter; the lock being mounted on the opposite side from that on the usual gun. The Spanish-style barrel carries London proof marks and is marked SANDWELL, MINORIES, LONDON. Circa 1760.

64. A double-barrelled flintlock sporting gun with browned Damascus barrels and marked (at the breech) BASS, a fine gunmaker. Circa 1775.

65. A French double-barrelled flintlock gun, the barrel bearing the mark of the barrelsmith Nicholas Le Clerc. The remainder of the gun was built by Chasteau of Paris whose name appears on the lock. The silver decoration carries the Paris hallmarks for 1772. The padded cheek piece is often found on Continental guns.

16

66. An English flintlock, breech-loading, sporting rifle, the barrel having ten-groove rifling. The rear sight is an integral part of a threaded plug which unscrews to give direct access to the breech for loading. The lock is signed NEWTON and has a push-on safety catch. Circa 1770.

67. A French repeating sporting gun with six rotating chambers each having an individual pan and frizzen. The back-action lock is signed CARREAUX and the swan-neck cock would have to be cocked before each shot. This type of multiple chambered flintlock was liable to a disconcerting and dangerous chain-fire if one chamber set off one or all of the others. Circa 1700.

68. This is the lock and breech section of a four-chambered sporting gun, each chamber being loaded separately and fitted with frizzen and spring. The catch just in front of the trigger guard unlocks the cylinder and allows the block to be rotated to bring each chamber into the firing position. Prior to each shot the action had to be cocked. The tang is marked LAZARINO COMINAZZO, a famed maker whose name was used by many others to persuade clients that the gun was of top quality. The trigger guard is signed CLAUDIO BARDIA and the gun dates from about 1780–90.

69. A late eighteenth century German, four-barrelled flintlock sporting gun, the Damascus barrels being circular with faceted breeches. Selection of barrels is made by sliding pan covers which expose the various vents. The locks are signed OFFERMAN LE JEUNE COLOGNE and are engraved with trophy. The stocks show typical Continental carving and decoration.

70. A Thuringian flintlock fowling piece with a Spanish-type barrel chiselled at the breech and signed IOH AND. KREUCHENREUTER. The lock is gilded and chiselled with stags and scrolls; the furniture is of gilt bronze. Third quarter of the eighteenth century.

71. A rare double-barrelled gun with one smooth and one rifled barrel, signed TATHAM LONDON in gold on strap. The breech has the royal coat of arms in gold, a platinum vent and gold-lined pan. The lock is unusual in having an externally-mounted mainspring. This is one of a group of guns intended for presentation to Red Indian chiefs as a mark of friendship and alliance with the British. Circa 1800.

72. Conventional double-barrelled Irish sporting gun with Damascus barrels signed McDERMOT DUBLIN. It is half stocked and has chequering at fore-end and grip. Circa 1820.

73. The advent of the percussion system caused many owners to have their favourite guns converted to it. This gun was originally a flintlock, but was adapted to take a pellet lock designed by Rivieres, a London maker. The circular-headed hammer, numbered '525', has six recesses each holding one pellet of fulminate which is struck against the nipple when the hammer swings forward. After each shot the disc is rotated to bring the next pellet in line with the nipple. The barrels are signed PARKER LONDON. The gun dates from the late eighteenth century, but the hammer conversion was introduced in about 1820.

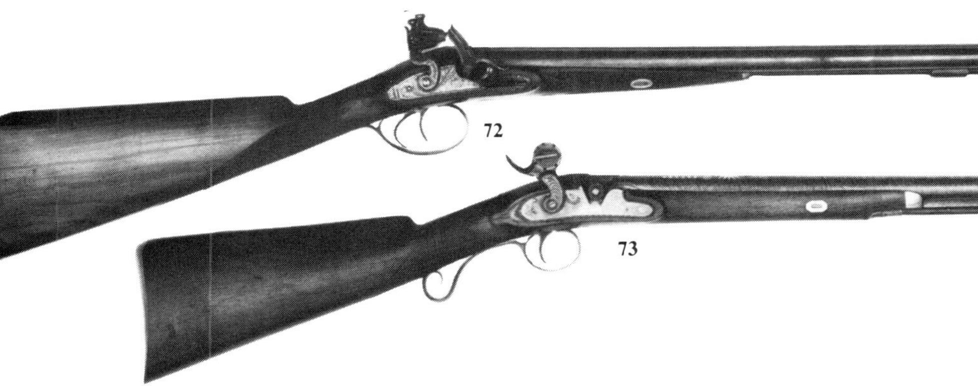

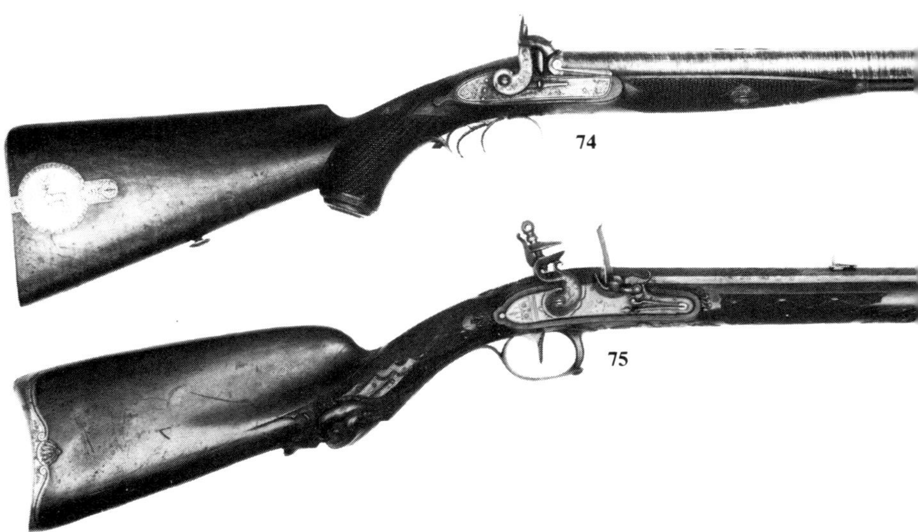

74. A double-barrelled rifle with two-groove rifled twist barrels signed CHARLES LANCASTER 151 NEW BOND STR. It has a three-leaf rear sight and the half stock has a pistol grip. The signed locks are fitted with front sliding bolt safety catches and the patchbox lid is engraved with a stag.

75. This early nineteenth century rifled carbine, with its blued octagonal barrel, was made by the famous French gunmaker Le Page of Paris.

76. This French sporting gun has another of the systems for feeding percussion pellets directly from a cylinder on to a nipple. The large drum has recesses for thirteen pellets and after each shot the drum was turned to bring the next recess into line with the nipple. The twist barrel is stamped IN V^{one} POTTET DELCUSSE and the cylinder or disc is signed BREVETE A PARIS. The barrel is secured to the breech by slots which engage with lugs on the breech, and to prevent loss of the barrel it was linked to the trigger guard – but the links are missing on this example. Circa 1820–30.

77. Sporting gun with Turkish barrel which is inlaid with chiselled gold and silver leaves. The lock, signed DIWISK,

is fitted with a Second Model Forsyth sliding primer which dropped small pellets into the touchhole each time the hammer was operated. Circa 1815.

78. A Scottish fowling piece with browned barrel of Spanish form, signed on the top flat of the octagonal breech WILLM HERIOT EDINBURGH. The lock and barrel are of the mid eighteenth century, but they were restocked in the early nineteenth century.

79. Double-barrelled sporting gun by Griffin & Tow of London, with gold vents, engraved locks and furniture. Circa 1775.

80. Silver-mounted, single-barrelled sporting gun; the Spanish-style barrel is signed W.BAILES LONDON on the breech. The locks have push-on safety bolts and are also signed. The silver lock plate and trigger guard carry hallmarks for 1763 and the maker's name, JEREMIAH ASHLEY.

81. Another silver-mounted fowling piece with genuine Spanish barrel by P. Estera. The locks are signed H.HADLEY and the silver furniture is hallmarked for 1764 and is also by Jeremiah Ashley.

76
77
78
79
80
81

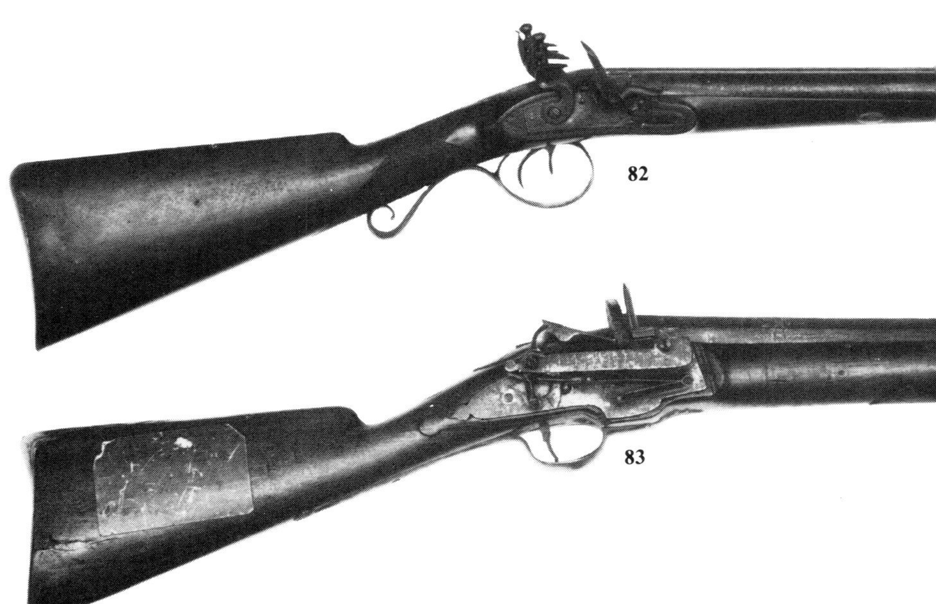

82. Double-barrelled sporting gun, the twist barrel having twin platinum lines at the breech, and a platinum vent; the locks and barrels signed LOTT OF READING. The pans are waterproof and have roller bearing frizzens. Circa 1820.

83. Although the stock is in the English style of the early eighteenth century, the barrel is Persian or Turkish and the gun has a large Miquelet lock. It was not at all uncommon for sportsmen to have foreign-made barrels, especially those from Spain or Turkey, mounted in a new stock for their use.

84. A Russian double-barrelled flintlock fowling piece, rather French in appearance, which was not unusual as the French gunmakers had a strong influence on Russian design. The locks are unusual being of screwless construction and are signed MYRAS. The metalwork has a frosted finish. Circa 1820.

85. Bohemian sporting gun with blued octagonal barrel and lock plate signed LEOPOLD BECKER (a maker in Carlsbad), full carved walnut stock. Circa 1745.

86. English fowling piece with browned twist barrel. The patent breech is signed NORTH WINTON on a gold plug. The furniture is blued and the half walnut stock is plain except for a small amount of chequering at the grip. Circa 1800.

87. German flintlock fowling piece, by Chretien Koerber of Ingelfingen, with silver inlaid oak leaves on the barrel. The stock is inlaid with silver studs and filigree work and the cheek rest has inlay of ebony and mother-of-pearl. Early nineteenth century.

88. Percussion-cap rifle, numbered '740', with Jacob's four-groove rifling, the barrel with top sighting flat signed ROBT.E.GARDEN 29 PICCADILLY LONDON; four-leaf sights, lock engraved and fitted with sliding safety bolt, finely figured walnut stock with silver escutcheon. Circa 1860.

89. Flintlock musketoon, with a three-stage barrel, the lock with sliding safety catch signed T.LONDON; brass furniture. Mid eighteenth century.

90. Single-barrelled, flintlock sporting gun, sighting rib on barrel, platinum vent, lock signed JOSEPH MANTON LONDON, circa 1810. This gun, numbered '5178', is believed to have belonged to Horace St. Paul, a Count of the Holy Roman Empire, who fought for Austria during the Seven Years War.

84
85
86
87
88
89
90

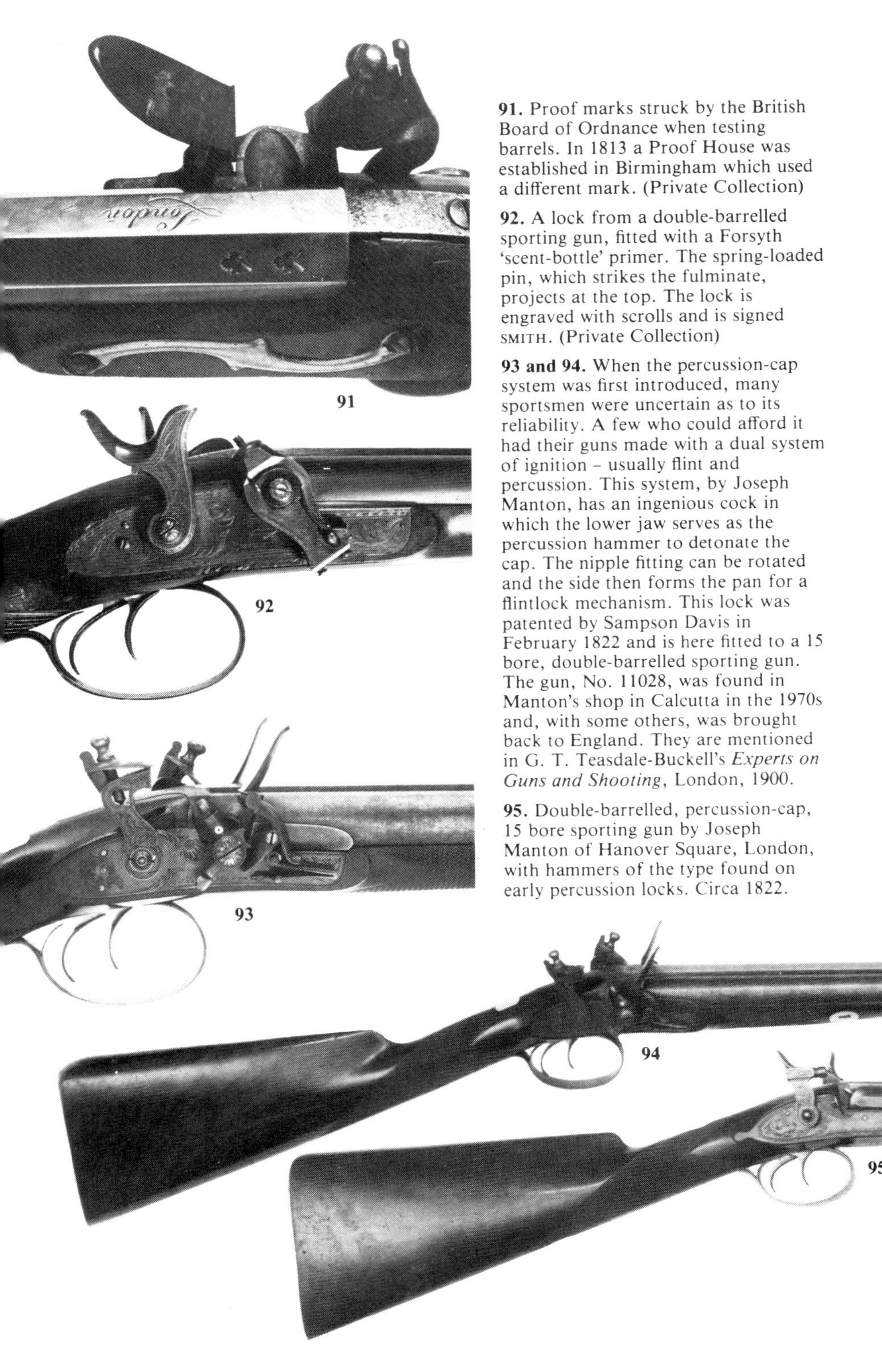

91. Proof marks struck by the British Board of Ordnance when testing barrels. In 1813 a Proof House was established in Birmingham which used a different mark. (Private Collection)

92. A lock from a double-barrelled sporting gun, fitted with a Forsyth 'scent-bottle' primer. The spring-loaded pin, which strikes the fulminate, projects at the top. The lock is engraved with scrolls and is signed SMITH. (Private Collection)

93 and 94. When the percussion-cap system was first introduced, many sportsmen were uncertain as to its reliability. A few who could afford it had their guns made with a dual system of ignition – usually flint and percussion. This system, by Joseph Manton, has an ingenious cock in which the lower jaw serves as the percussion hammer to detonate the cap. The nipple fitting can be rotated and the side then forms the pan for a flintlock mechanism. This lock was patented by Sampson Davis in February 1822 and is here fitted to a 15 bore, double-barrelled sporting gun. The gun, No. 11028, was found in Manton's shop in Calcutta in the 1970s and, with some others, was brought back to England. They are mentioned in G. T. Teasdale-Buckell's *Experts on Guns and Shooting*, London, 1900.

95. Double-barrelled, percussion-cap, 15 bore sporting gun by Joseph Manton of Hanover Square, London, with hammers of the type found on early percussion locks. Circa 1822.

96. One of a pair of 18 bore, percussion-cap guns also by Joseph Manton. The barrels have platinum vents. This metal, first used early in the nineteenth century, became the most common anti-corrosive metal used in the manufacture of locks. Circa 1821.

97. A double-barrelled Needham's Patent, breech-loading sporting gun, breech inscribed PATENT LONDON NO.1116. The action was operated by a lever which was raised to allow the breech to swing out sideways and to cock the hammers. The patent was granted in October 1852 and was designed for a centre-fire cartridge.

98. A four-shot, double-barrelled, superimposed load sporting gun with twist barrels. The locks are so made that the first pressure releases the front hammer, and second pressure the rear hammer. The patent was granted in 1842 to two Liège designers. Mid nineteenth century.

99. A 10-shot, 11mm, pinfire rifle, the barrel inscribed LEFAUCHEUX INVᵗ BREVETE. The stock is profusely inlaid with silver wire and the frame and cylinder are engraved with scrolls. The hammer is cocked by pressure on the trigger and the weapon carries Liège proof marks. (Christies)

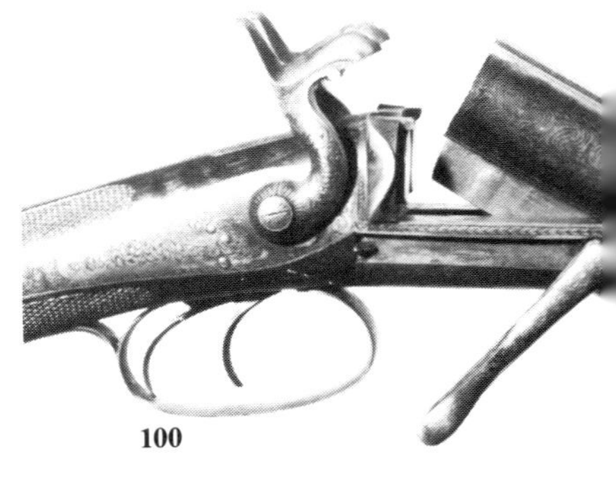

100. A double-barrelled, pinfire 'Lockfast' gun, No. 2011, a design patented in May 1860 by James Dalziell Dougall. The operation of the side lever moved the barrels forward to disengage them before being tilted for ejection and reloading. The Damascus barrels are browned, and the frame is engraved with scrolls. Dougall was a Scottish gunmaker who was well known to sportsmen of the period as a contributor to shooting magazines and the author of several books. (Christies)

100

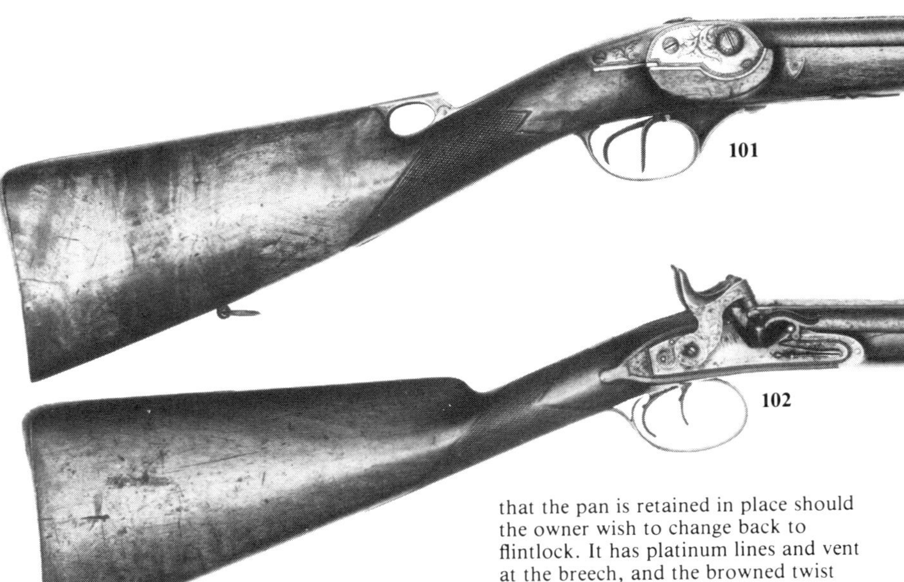

101

102

101. A French, double-barrelled, breech-loading sporting gun, signed J A ROBERT BREVETE A PARIS in gold on the Damascus barrels. This gun used a metal cartridge with the priming in the rim and was patented in 1831. The breech was opened by means of the ringed lever set along the top of the butt. The frame is engraved with scrolls and EXPOSITION DE 1834 ACADEMIE DE L'INDUSTRIE SOCIETE D'ENCOURAGE-MENT.

102. English, double-barrelled, percussion-cap gun, ingeniously converted from flintlock in such a way that the pan is retained in place should the owner wish to change back to flintlock. It has platinum lines and vent at the breech, and the browned twist barrels are signed JOSEPH MANTON HANOVER SQUARE LONDON in gold. Early nineteenth century.

103. This page from a nineteenth-century book on gunmaking shows some of the various Damascus patterns produced by combinations of metal ribbons and twists. (Private Collection)

104 and 105. A Scottish, mid nineteenth century, double-barrelled, percussion-cap sporting gun of typical design, with finely engraved locks signed J.D.DOUGALL, half-stocked with chequering at the grip. The barrels are Damascus and show clearly the pattern produced by the twisting and folding of the ribbons of iron and steel.

Fig. 183.—Gun-Barrel Iron, Twisted, and laid into a Riband.

Fig. 184.—Two-Iron Damascus Barrel.

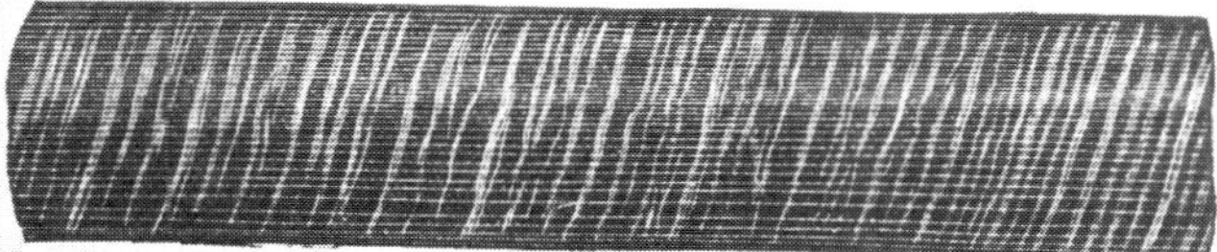

Fig. 184a.—Scelp Gun-Barrel.

Fig. 185.—Three-Iron-Steel Damascus Barrel.

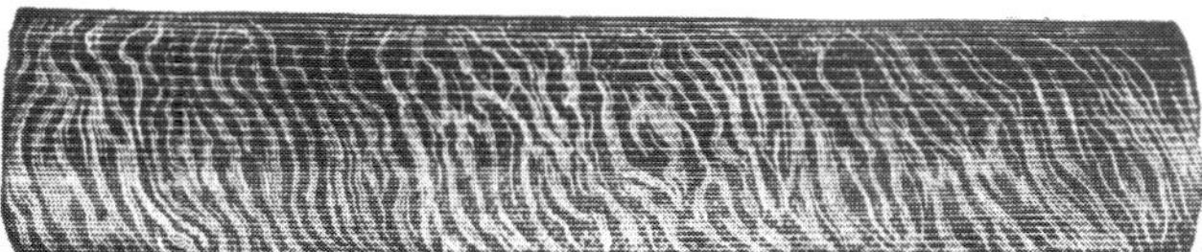

Fig. 185a.—Single-Iron Damascus Barrel.

103.

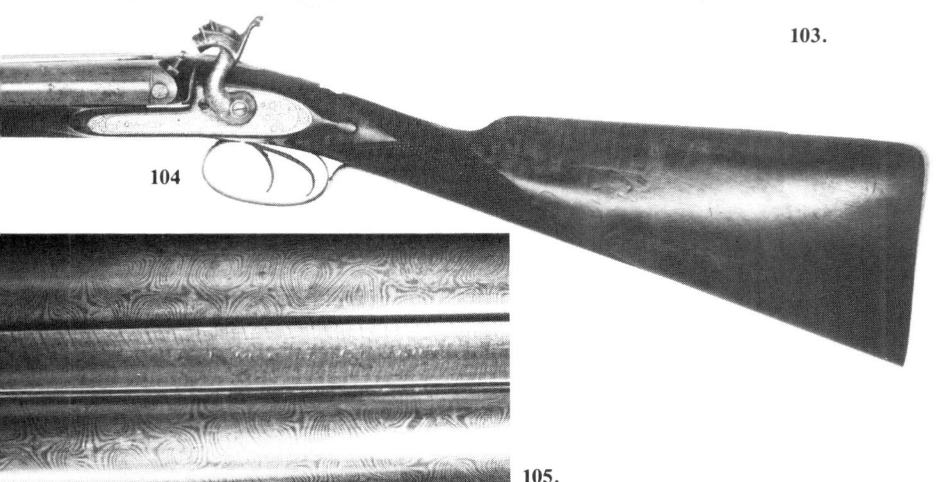

104

105.

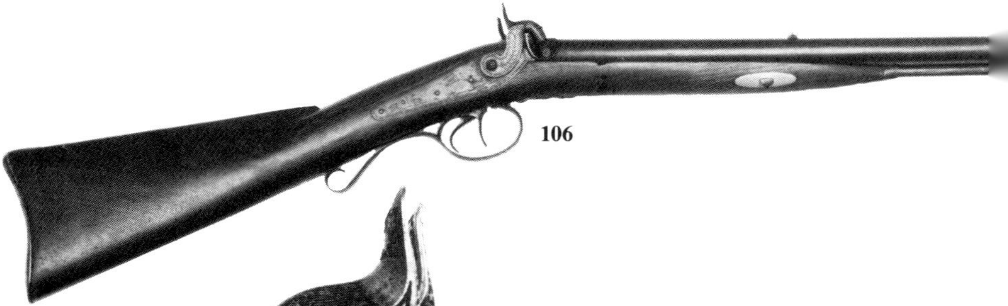

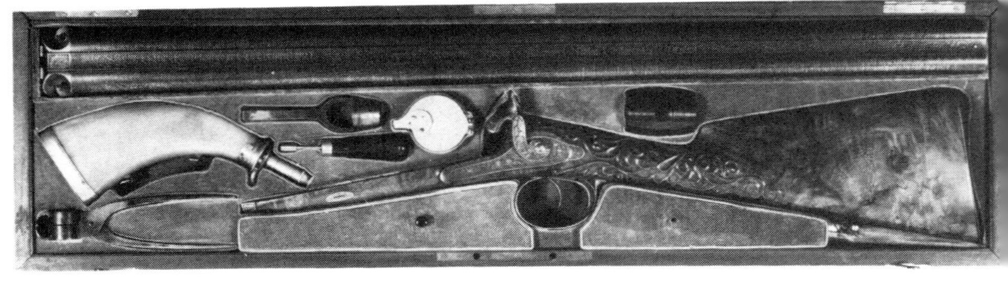

106

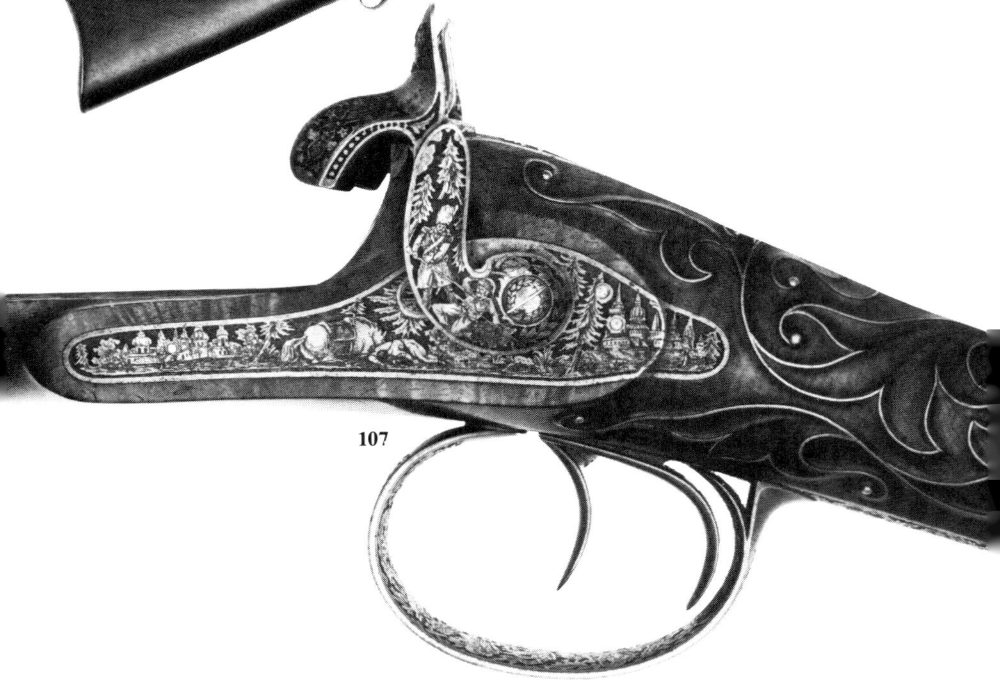

107

108

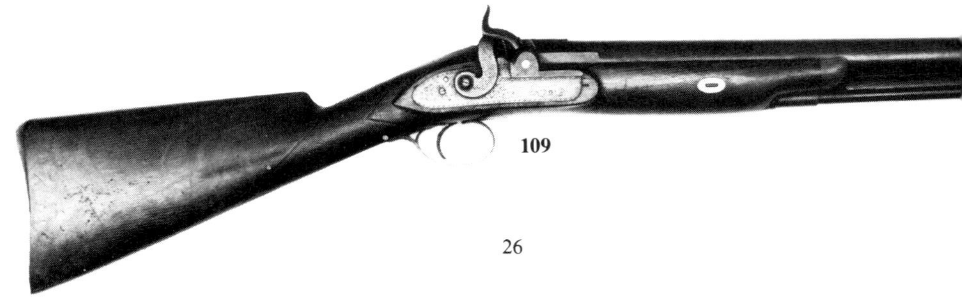

109

26

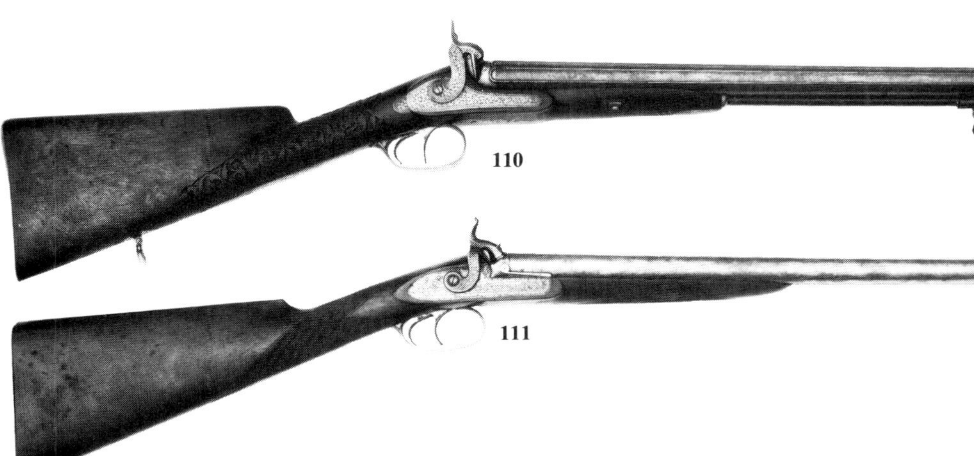

106. A double-barrelled percussion rifle made in the USA in about 1860, and signed B MILLS RAMITON UC on the rib. It has engraved back-action locks and a scrolled trigger guard typical of those found on many rifles.

107 and 108. A highly decorated, double-barrelled, French fowling piece with Damascus barrels, the rib signed LEPAGE ARQER DU ROY AT S.A. LE PRINCE ROYALE. The locks and hammers are chiselled with military scenes showing the French in action in Egypt and Russia. A walnut half stock has steel wire scrolling inlay and the butt plate is inscribed H LEPAGE FILS DE J LEPAGE AQER DU IR CONSUL ARQER DE L'EMPEREUR. The gun and its accessories, including cap dispenser, wad-cutter, mould, nipple key and powder flask, is housed in a velvet-lined contoured case – the whole dating from circa 1845.

109. A single-barrelled, 6 bore wild-fowling gun, the Damascus barrel browned to reduce rusting, and signed WESTLEY RICHARDS 170 NEW BOND ST. LONDON. The walnut half stock has a chequered grip. The gun dates from the middle of the nineteenth century.

110. Belgian, double-barrelled, 12 bore, percussion-cap sporting gun, signed M.J. CHAUMONT, FOURNISSEUR DU ROI DU PAYS BAS in gold along the rib. The barrels are stamped with Liège proof marks and the locks and hammers are engraved with scrolls. As with many Continental guns there are swivels for the fitting of a sling. Circa 1855.

111. Designed for shooting at live pigeons released from traps, and made by one of the most famous London makers, Purdey of Oxford Street. It has platinum vents and the only decoration is some restrained engraving on the locks. Circa 1860.

112. A fine cased, four-barrel percussion gun, made by Charles Lancaster in about 1840. The Damascus barrels have sights set up to 300 yards and fire a .500 ball; they could be rotated to bring each pair into the firing position. The case contains all the accessories including bullet mould, powder flask, wad-cutter, cleaning rods and various tools.

112.

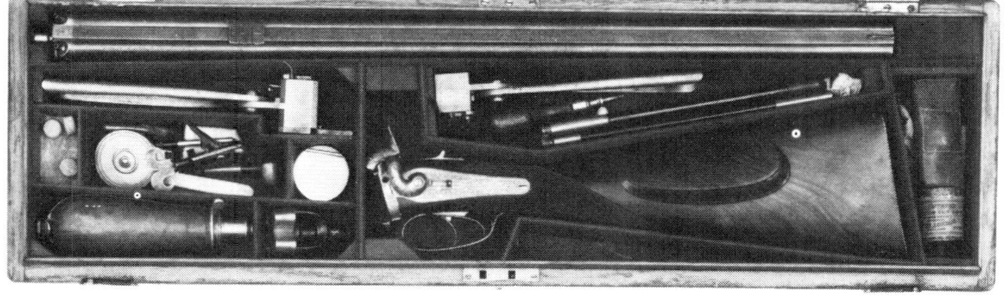

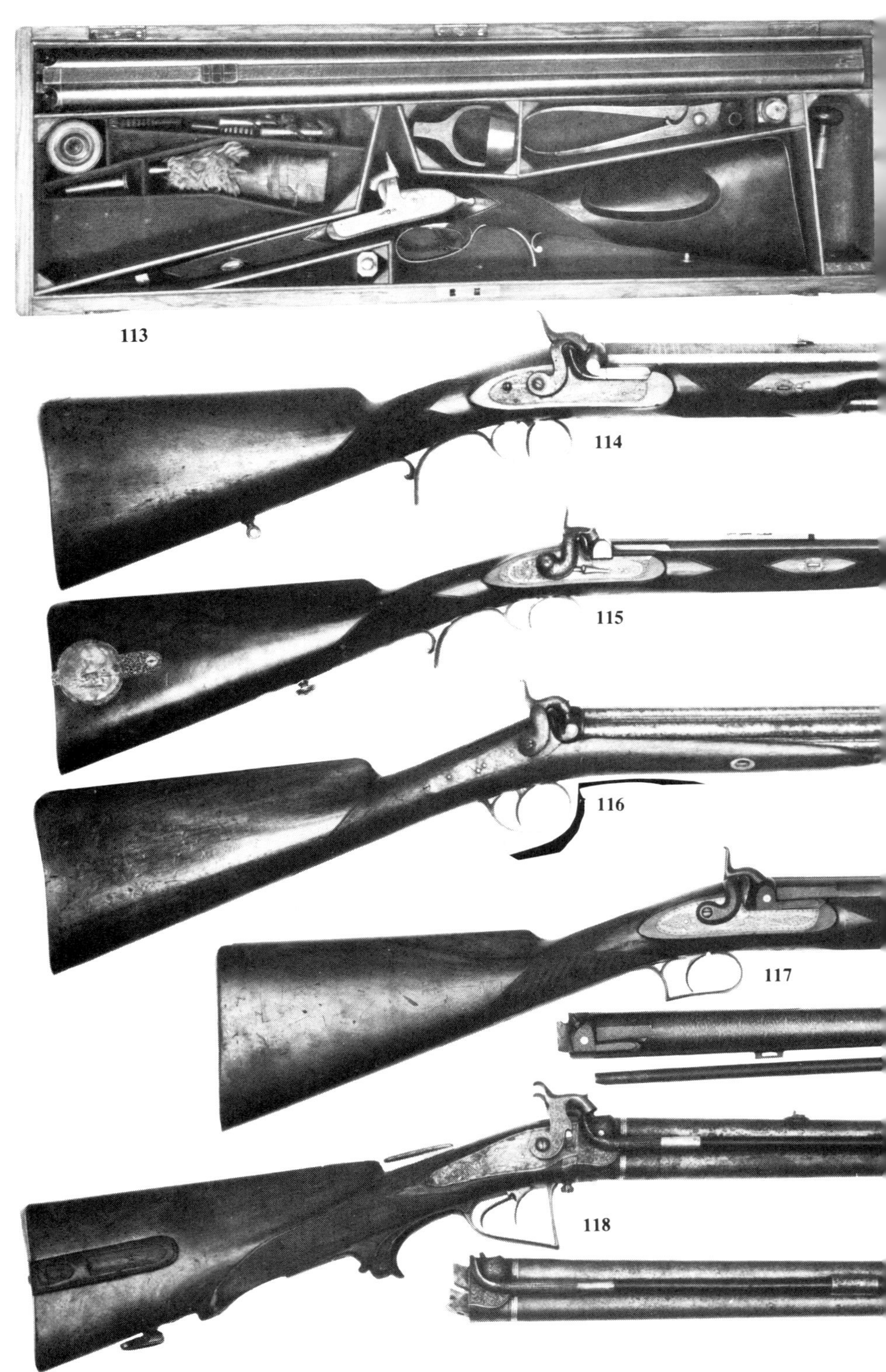
113
114
115
116
117
118

113. A cased, 10 bore, double-barrelled percussion gun by Charles Lancaster of 151 New Bond Street, London – one barrel smooth bored, the other rifled with leaf sights up to 300 yards and with gilt furniture. The locks are signed LANCASTER LONDON and the gun is numbered '3727'. The accessories include a bullet mould, wad-cutter, cap box and various cleaning tools.

114. A 4 bore sporting gun with octagonal barrel and half stock by JAMES BURROW OF 116 FISHERGATE, PRESTON, engraved lock with sliding safety.

115. A rifle designed primarily for target work, with six-groove rifling and signed WHITWORTH PATENT NO.271 at the breech. Made in about 1860. Sir Joseph Whitworth, born 1803, became one of the leading experimenters in the effects of rifling and was responsible for the use of hexagonal rifling. He was also responsible for improvements in the design of steel barrels for shotguns. He died in 1887.

116. Seven-barrelled percussion rifle, No. 3476, by FORSYTH & CO., PATENT GUN MAKER LONDON. It has a back-action lock and is half stocked.

117. Many regular shooters used a pair of guns to lessen wear on barrels, but others used one stock with interchangeable barrels as on this 8 bore, single-barrelled percussion gun. The Damascus barrel with London proof marks is signed JAMES SQUIRES (GUNMAKER) 12 CASTLE STREET, WHITECHAPEL, LONDON. The signed lock is engraved with a shooter and his dog. Circa 1860.

118. Austrian over-and-under gun with two sets of barrels, one set smooth the other with multi-groove rifling. The stock is carved with a simple pistol grip and there is a special grip safety fitted at the tang which prevents the gun from being fired unless the safety bar is depressed. The maker was Mathias Nowotny of Vienna. Circa 1850.

119 and 120. A German Schutzen, or target rifle, fitted with heavy, octagonal, multi-grooved rifled barrel and decorated with panels of gold damascening. The barrels are signed B.A.DIRKU JUNIOR and ENGL: GUSS ≡ STAHL, locks and hammers are chiselled with scrolls and locks inscribed IN REICHENBERG. The full stock has nickel silver mounts and is inlaid with panels of mother-of-pearl and ivory straps, and the butt has an inlay of Diana and a hound. This is unusually ornate and may well have been made as a presentation or prize weapon.

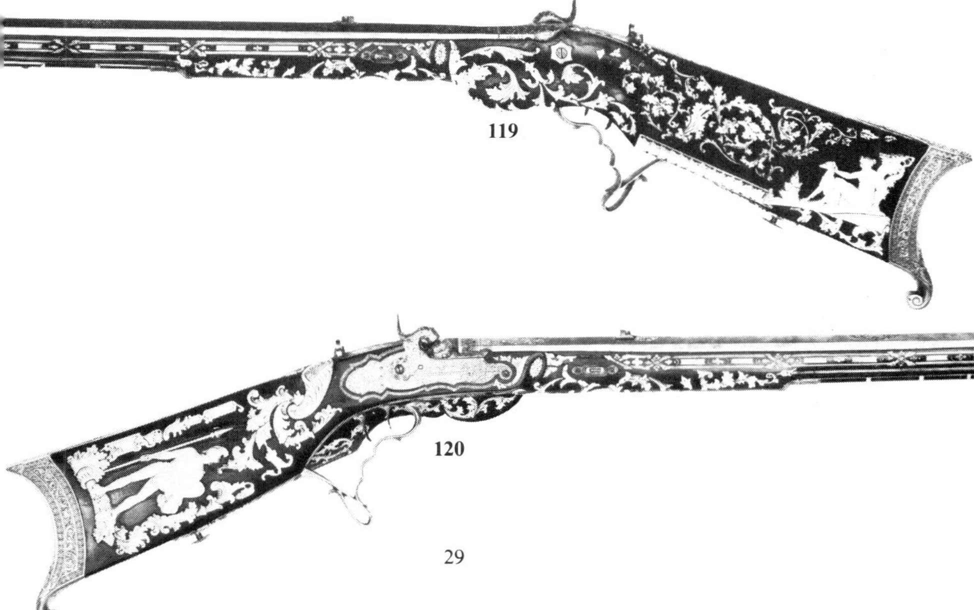

119

120

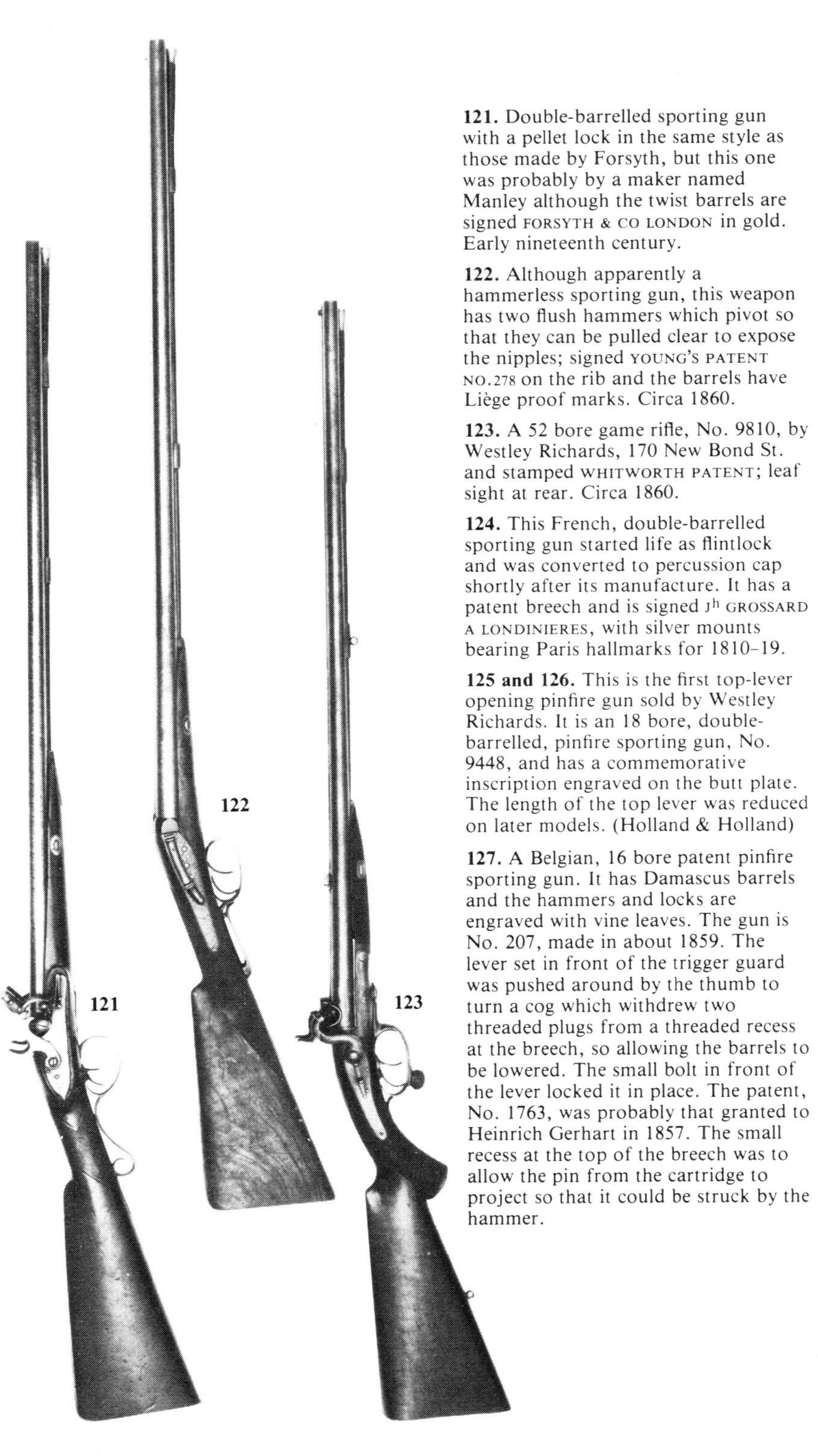

121. Double-barrelled sporting gun with a pellet lock in the same style as those made by Forsyth, but this one was probably by a maker named Manley although the twist barrels are signed FORSYTH & CO LONDON in gold. Early nineteenth century.

122. Although apparently a hammerless sporting gun, this weapon has two flush hammers which pivot so that they can be pulled clear to expose the nipples; signed YOUNG'S PATENT NO.278 on the rib and the barrels have Liège proof marks. Circa 1860.

123. A 52 bore game rifle, No. 9810, by Westley Richards, 170 New Bond St. and stamped WHITWORTH PATENT; leaf sight at rear. Circa 1860.

124. This French, double-barrelled sporting gun started life as flintlock and was converted to percussion cap shortly after its manufacture. It has a patent breech and is signed J^h GROSSARD A LONDINIERES, with silver mounts bearing Paris hallmarks for 1810–19.

125 and 126. This is the first top-lever opening pinfire gun sold by Westley Richards. It is an 18 bore, double-barrelled, pinfire sporting gun, No. 9448, and has a commemorative inscription engraved on the butt plate. The length of the top lever was reduced on later models. (Holland & Holland)

127. A Belgian, 16 bore patent pinfire sporting gun. It has Damascus barrels and the hammers and locks are engraved with vine leaves. The gun is No. 207, made in about 1859. The lever set in front of the trigger guard was pushed around by the thumb to turn a cog which withdrew two threaded plugs from a threaded recess at the breech, so allowing the barrels to be lowered. The small bolt in front of the lever locked it in place. The patent, No. 1763, was probably that granted to Heinrich Gerhart in 1857. The small recess at the top of the breech was to allow the pin from the cartridge to project so that it could be struck by the hammer.

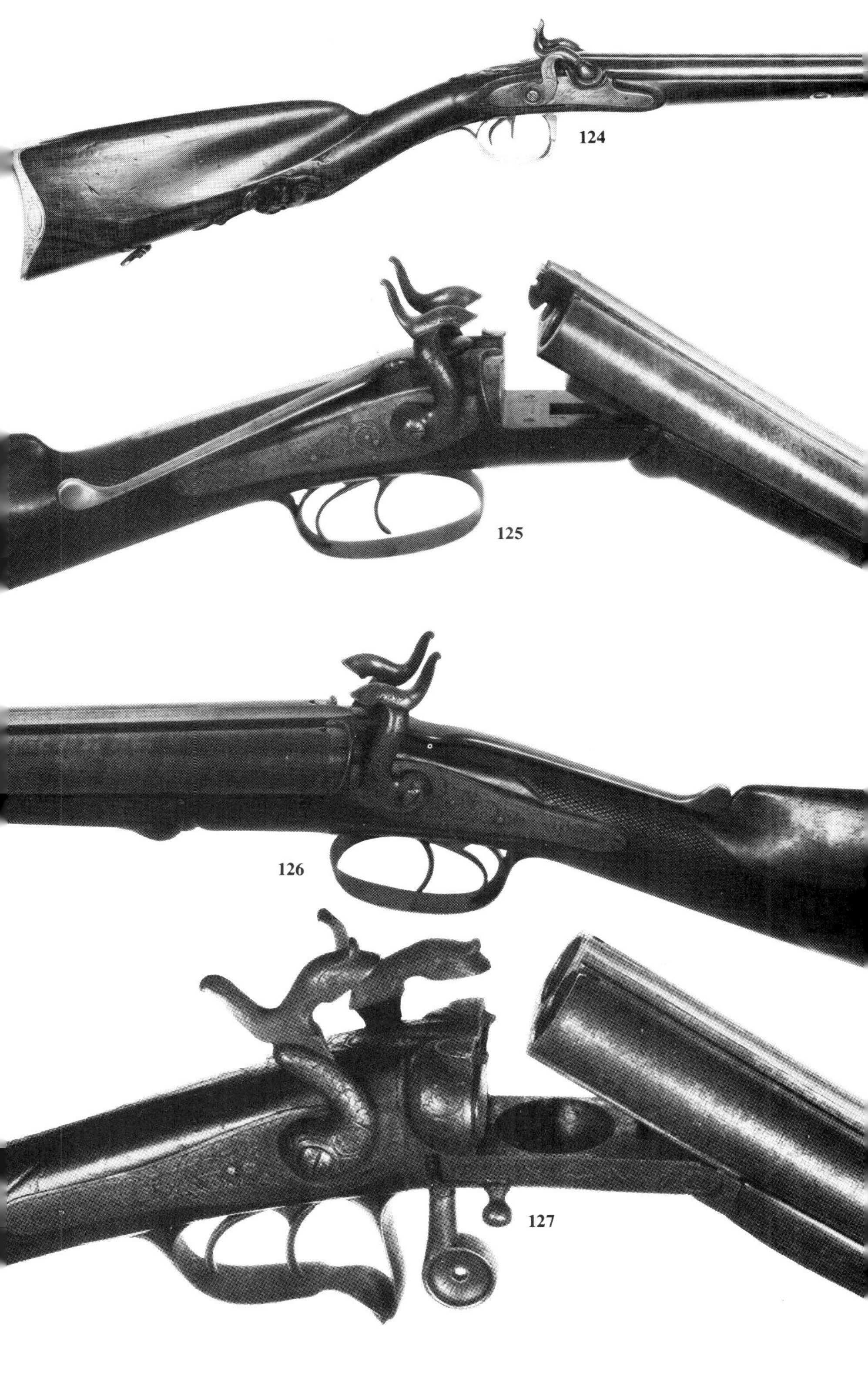

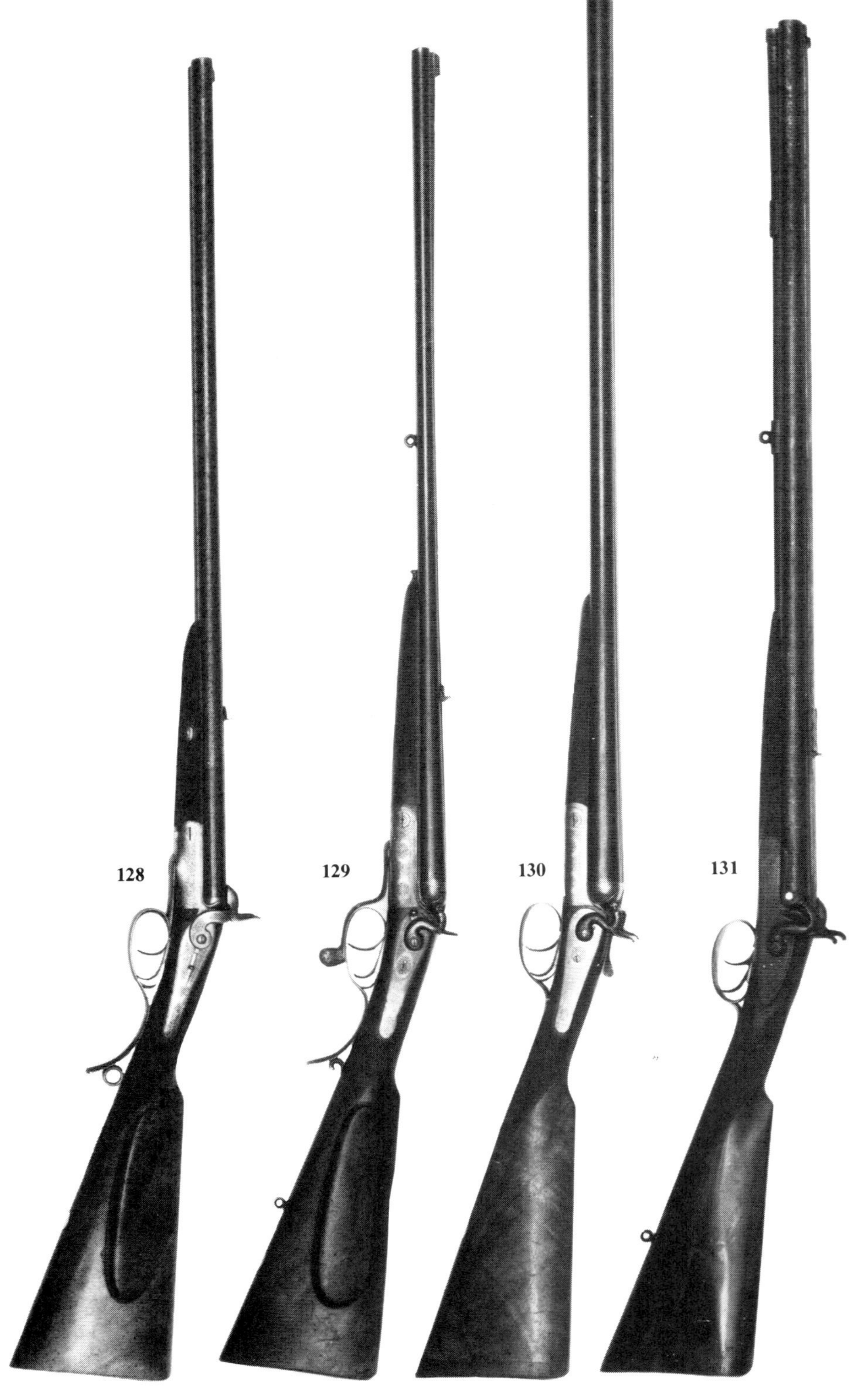
128
129
130
131

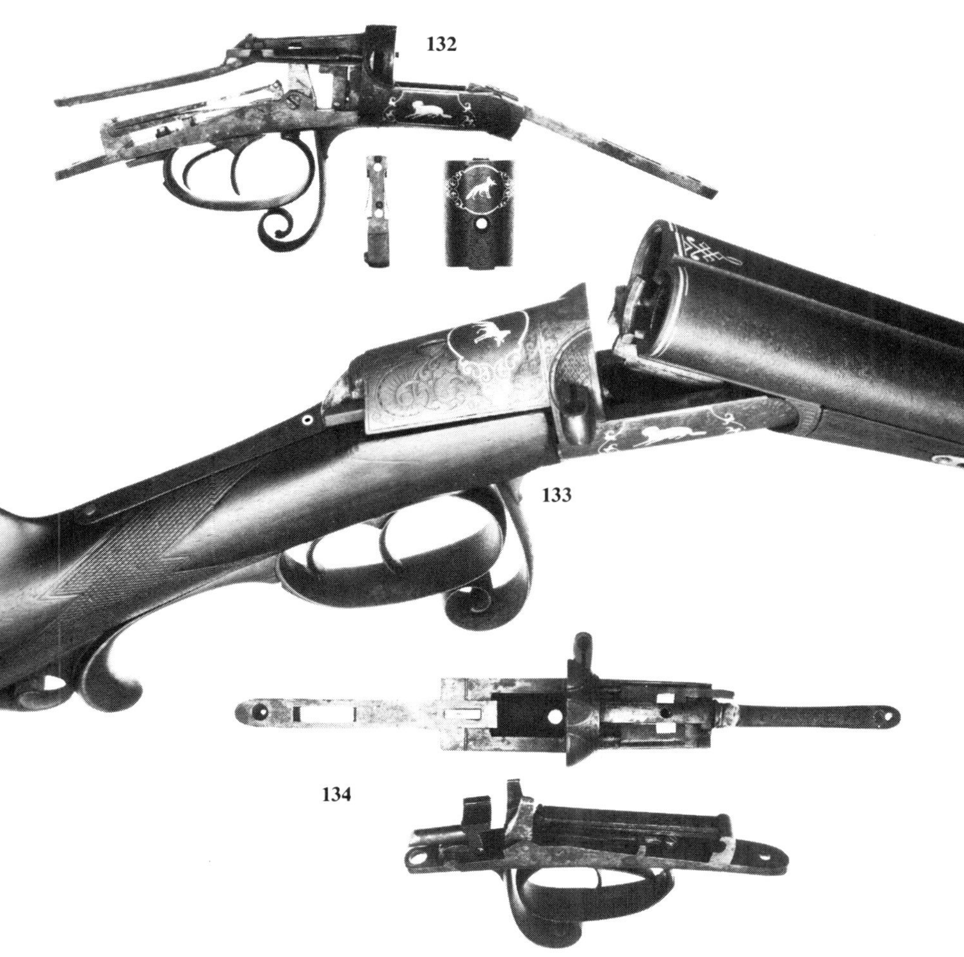

128. A 38 bore, pinfire rifle, No. 6473, by J. Purdey, leaf sights up to 200 yards. Circa 1860.

129. .303 non-ejector hammer rifle, No. 17020, by J. Purdey & Sons. Whitworth fluid-pressed steel barrels, leaf sights to 250 yards. Bears monogram of His Grace the Duke of Fife.

130. 12 bore, double-barrelled, ejector, self-opening sporting gun with top lever, also by J. Purdey & Sons, also with Whitworth fluid-pressed steel barrels. Made in 1899 for the Earl of Ava.

131. 16 bore percussion-cap rifle, Damascus barrels signed C.P. SWINBURN & SON MAKERS, Birmingham proof marks. Circa 1860.

132, 133 and 134. The London gunmaker G. H. Daw was for long credited with the introduction of the hammerless gun in 1862. There is reason to doubt this; there being evidence to indicate that guns of this design were in use in Prussia prior to that date. This decorative, double-barrelled gun is an example of what are usually described as 'Daw's Hammerless'. The vertical arms which power the firing pins can be seen in the dismantled lock. (Christies)

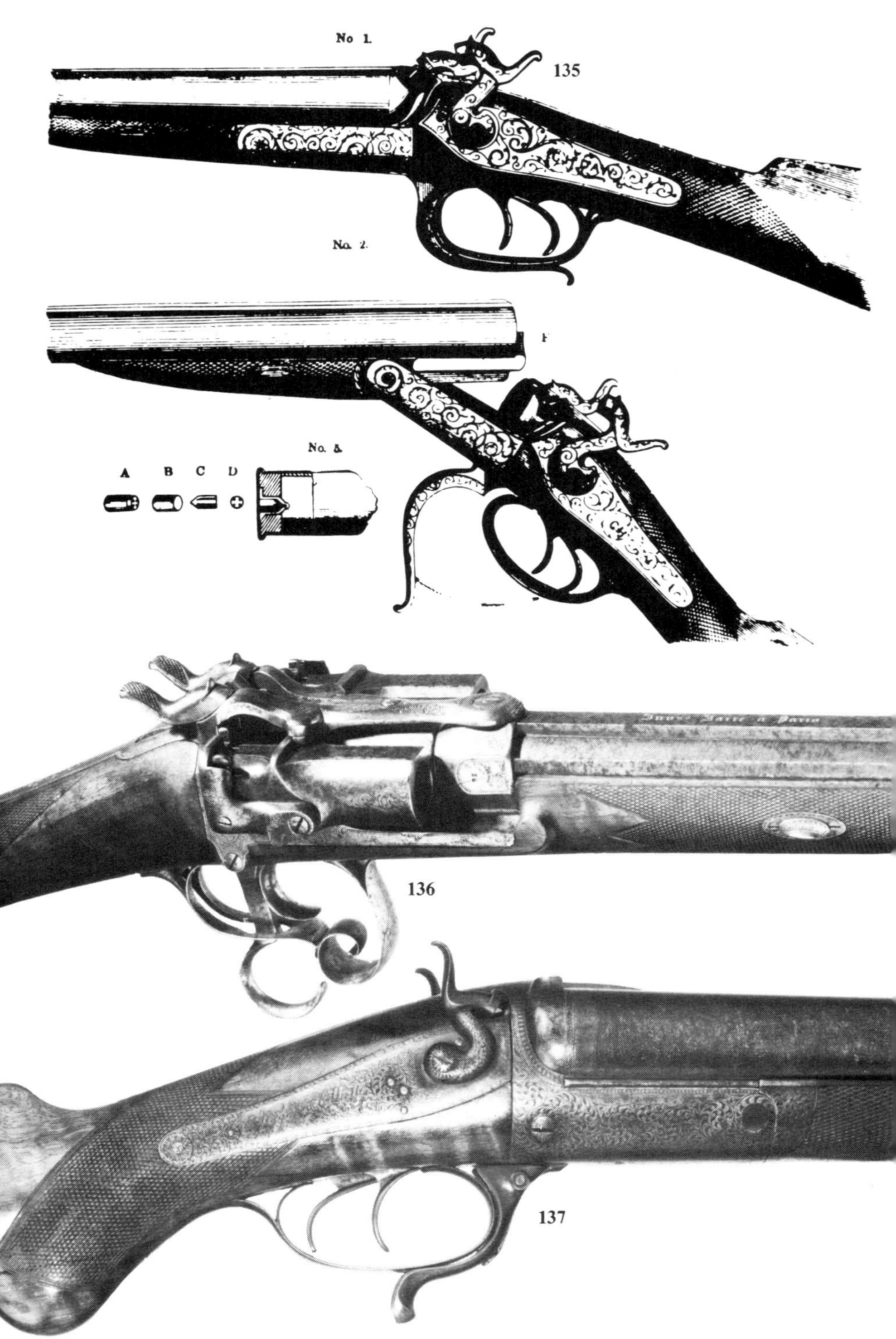

No 1.
135
No 2.
No 3.
A B C D
136
137

135. Contemporary illustration of one of the earliest centrefire breech-loading sporting guns by George Daw, one of the pioneers of modern firearms design. No. 1, closed for firing; No. 2, open for loading; No. 5, section of cartridge, showing the central-fire in the charge; A, cap on anvil, showing the end that rests on the powder; B, percussion cap; C, the anvil; D, end view of the anvil.

136. In 1873 a patent was granted to A.E. & P.H. Jarre for this unusual gun which uses a horizontal, four-chambered magazine. The magazine has a hinged backplate which allows access for the pinfire cartridge. Operation of the long, rear 'trigger' moves the magazine which is then held in position ready for firing. This example has the rib signed INV⸍ JARRE A PARIS in gold.

137. In 1866 the British sporting magazine *The Field* held a trial to settle the controversy about the performance of breech-loading and muzzle-loading sporting guns. This patent snap-action under-lever 8 bore hammer gun by

Elliott, No. 2949, the rib signed ELLIOTTS' PATENT WIGGAN COMPANY MAKERS, dating from about 1865, could well have been one of the guns entered in the trial. It has been re-stocked.

138. In 1879 *The Field* held another trial and this 20 bore, double-barrelled gun by W. W. Greener, No. 19268, was one of the entries. The silver-plated barrels are inscribed THE WINNING GUN AT THE LONDON GUN TRIALS 1879. Despite the inscription the printed results indicate that Greener's gun came only second in Class 3. (Christies)

139. A double-barrelled, 8 bore hammer gun by W. W. Greener, No. 34433, with 32in barrels and back-action locks. The barrels opened by operating the under-lever. The metal-work has only a minimum of engraved decoration.

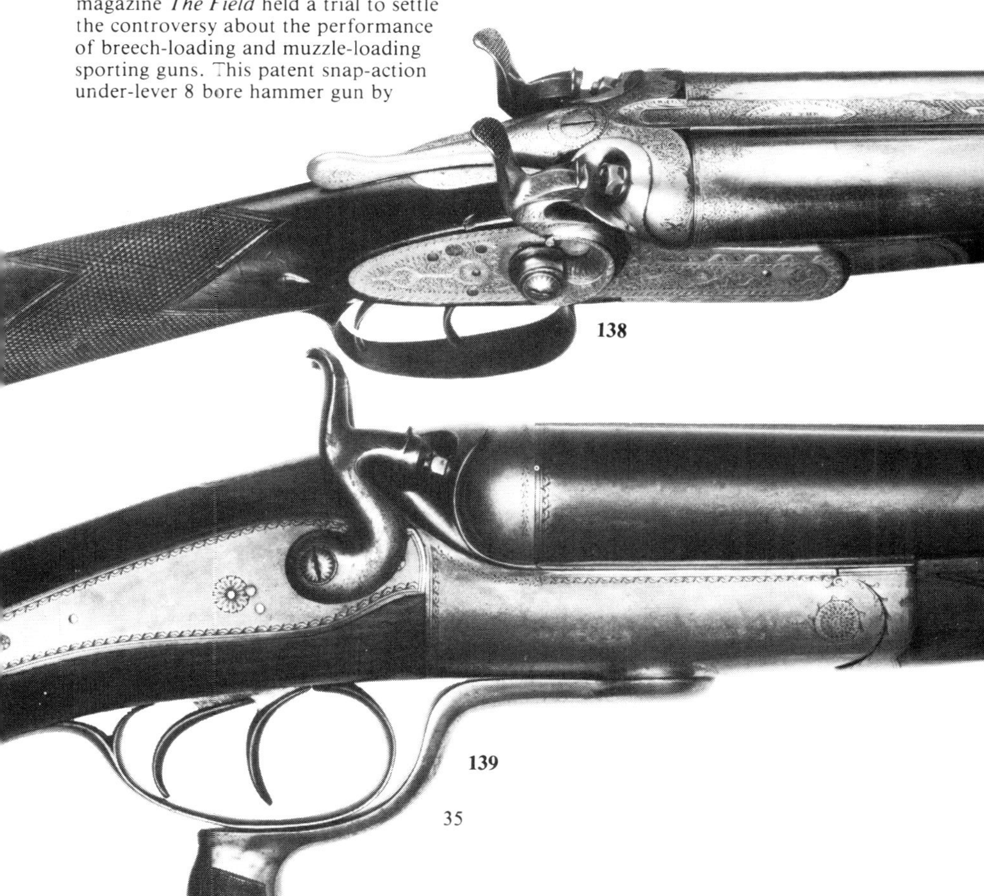

138

139

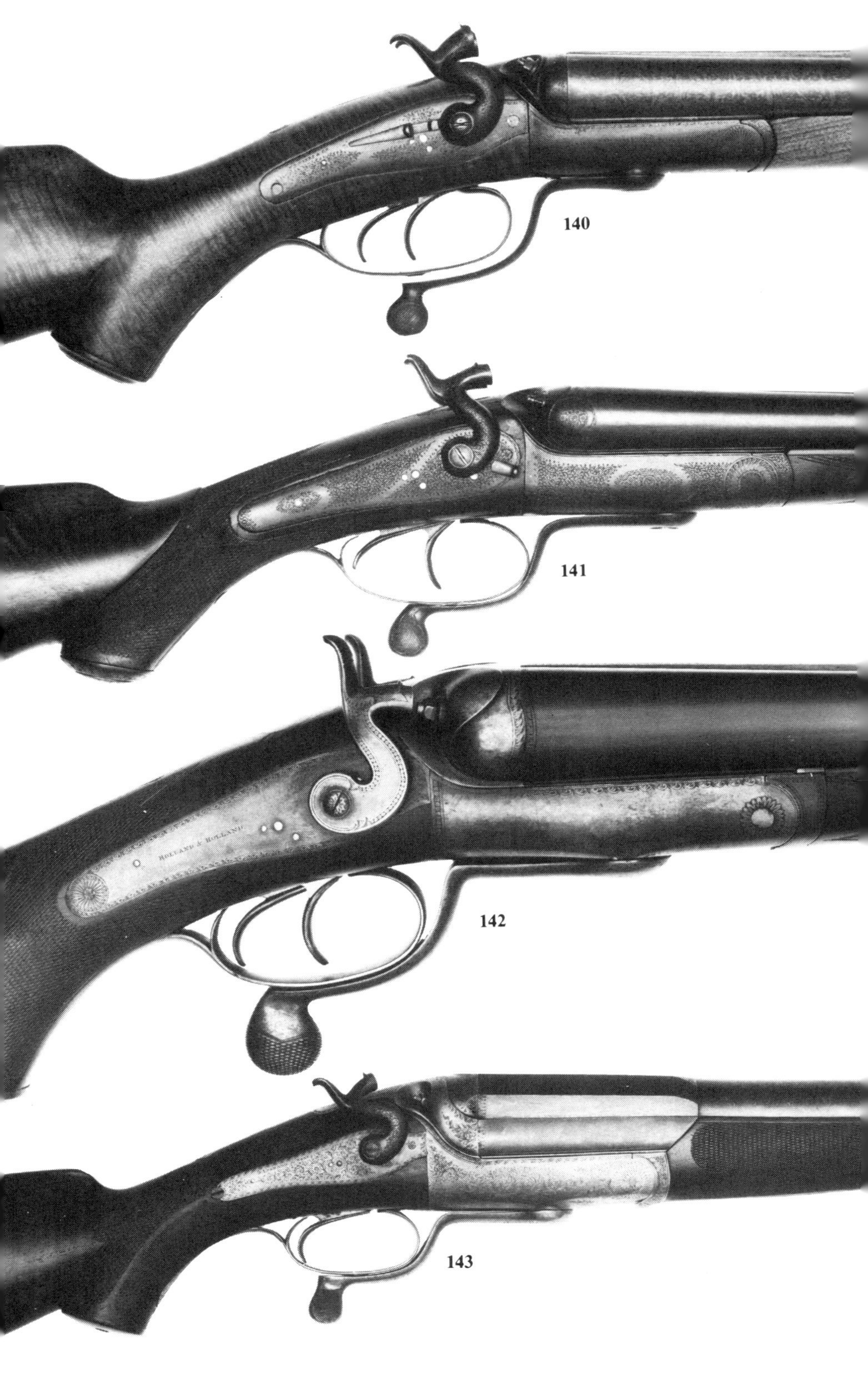
140
141
142
143

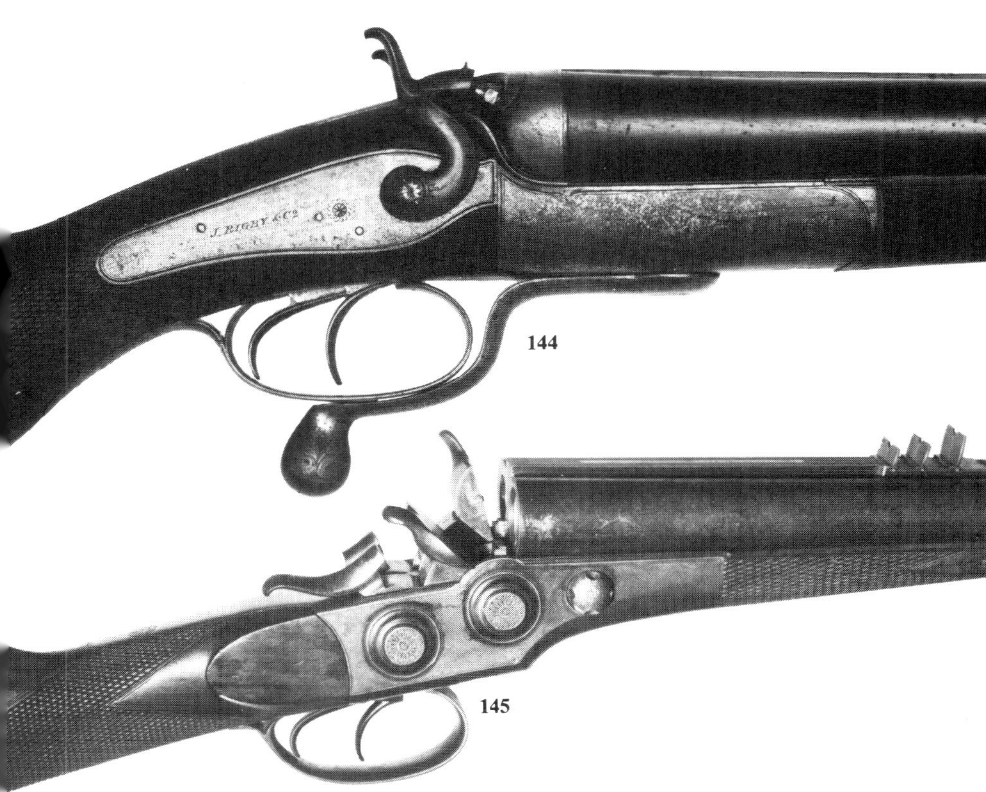

144

145

140. 39 bore, double-barrelled, non-ejector game rifle, No. 21399, by R. B. Rodda & Co. 25¾in Damascus barrels, leaf sights to 200 yards, back-action locks with rebounding hammers. The back-action lock also has sliding bolt safety catches to lock the hammers in a 'safe' position. The finely figured stock has a pistol grip as have most game rifles.

141. Another under-lever hammer gun, 38 bore, No. 11404, by J. Purdey & Sons. The locks have safety catches, but unlike most guns they are set in front of the hammer. The pistol grip is chequered to ensure a firmer grip. The engraving is of very good quality as befits one of the top gunmakers in the country.

142. An 8 bore, double-barrelled hammer gun, No. 15054, by Holland & Holland, another of the top gunmakers. This gun is a non-ejector which might make it a little less desirable for some keen shooters. Decoration is limited to a small amount of border engraving.

143. A 4 bore, single-barrelled, wildfowling gun by D. Leonard & Sons. Designed to take a 4in cartridge, the breech is strengthened to withstand the high pressures generated by such a big charge. Decorated with foliate scroll engraving.

144. An 8 bore, double-barrelled, non-ejector hammer gun for wildfowling, No. 8654 by J. Rigby & Co. The small side plate has only an engraved line border; under-lever opening.

145. In 1863 Leonard Ceiger obtained a patent (US 37501) for a breech-loading system known as the rolling block. When the gun action was cocked a block rolled back to give access to the breech; as the hammer descended the block was locked in position. This action is fitted on the Cape rifle and gun which has one 14 bore and one .450 rifled barrel. The weapon is engraved J.GRAINGER & SON (PATENTEES) GRAHAMSTOWN. Circa 1870–5. It is very unusual to find the rolling-block mechanism on double-barrelled guns. (Christies)

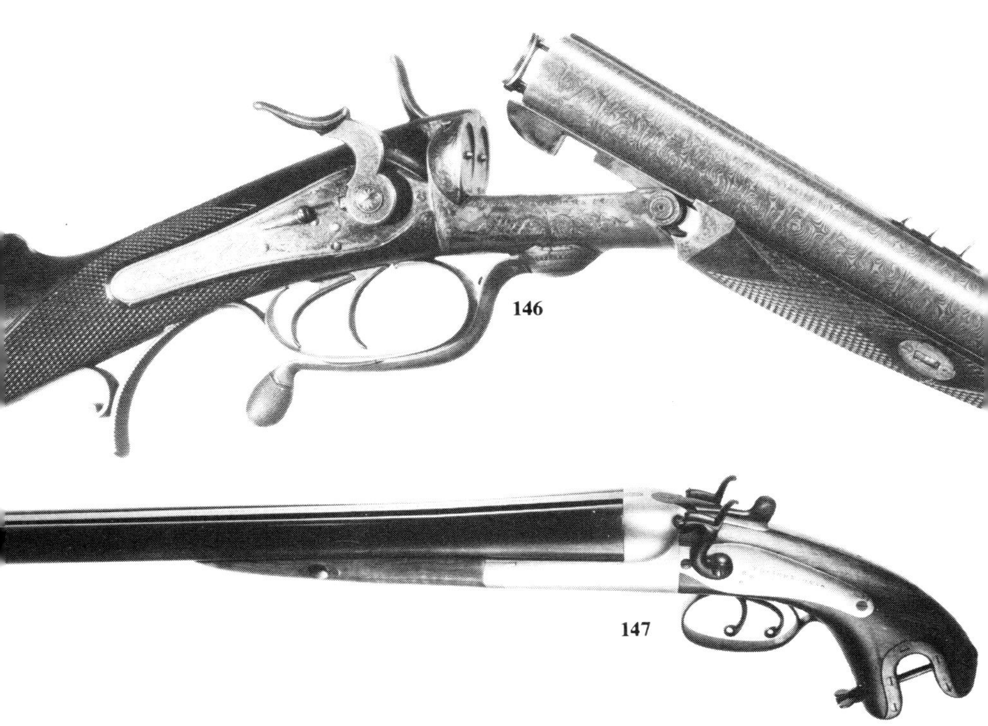

146. A 14 bore, double-barrelled, oval bore hammer gun, No. 4126, by C. Lancaster, based on a patent granted to Louis Gastinne in 1853. The under-lever activates a cam which moves the barrels backwards and forwards and so engages or releases a lug from the standing breech. Made in 1867, the fine pattern of the Damascus barrel is clearly visible. (Christies)

147. Slightly unusual 4 bore punt or wildfowler's gun, No. 17294, by Thomas Bland & Sons, with top lever opening and fitted with rebounding hammers. The gun is proved for nitro powder and has triggers with ringed tips. In place of a conventional butt, it has a truncated stock with a steel-lined recess for securing to a support.

148. A double-barrelled, .577 Express rifle – the barrels by Thomas Bland & Sons, the remainder of the weapon by J. Purdey, the whole slightly worn. The bar locks have push-on safety catches and the hammers are non-rebounding, i.e. they are not partly re-cocked when fired. No. 5277. Instead of a pistol grip the stock has a scrolled trigger guard to offer a firmer hold.

149. Although this 12 bore, non-ejector, side-lever hammer gun was made by T. Horsley it has Damascus barrels signed by J & W Tolley. The stock is chequered and the locks and hammers are engraved with foliate scrolls.

150. The opening lever on this 12 bore, double-barrelled sporting gun, No. 4185, is mounted above the stock, a system adopted by the makers of most modern sporting guns. The gun has, presumably, seen much service, because the original barrels have been replaced by a pair by Rowland Watson although the gun was made by Boss & Co., another outstanding gunmaker. The action is fitted with Boss patent ejectors. Originally proved only for black powder, the barrels have been re-proved for nitro cartridges, an uncommon feature on hammer guns.

151. A 12 bore, double-barrelled, non-ejector hammer gun, No. 6849 by Edwinson Green. This gun has also been rebarrelled and the engraving is good but restrained. Edwinson Green made and supplied guns to a number of different gunmakers.

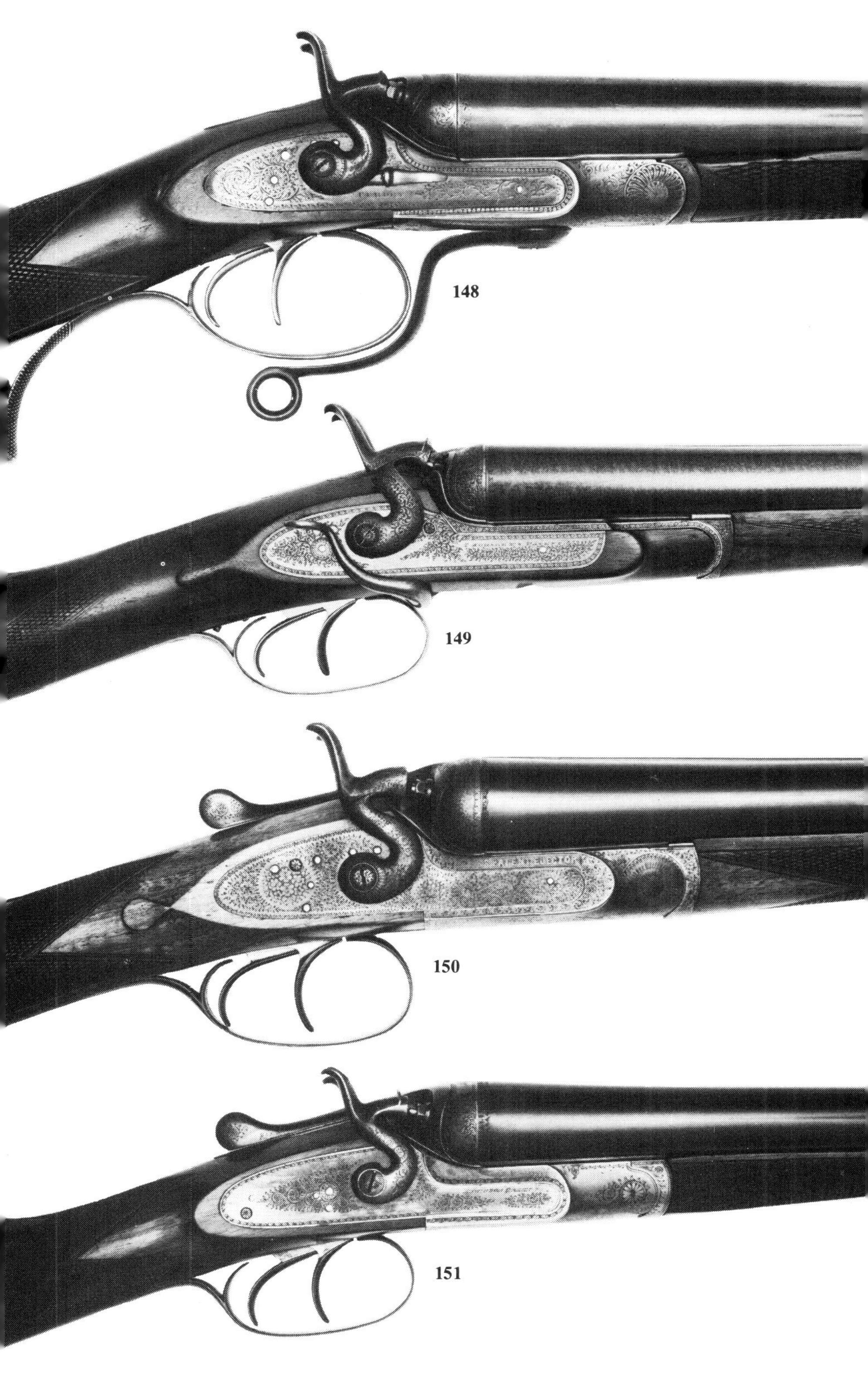

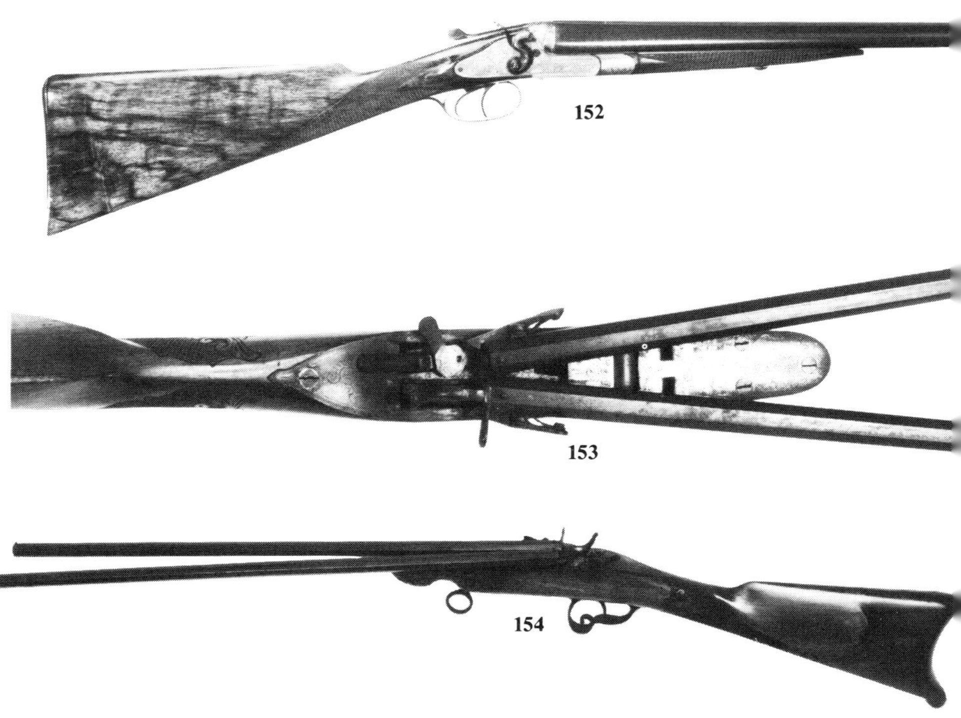

152

153

154

152. Although apparently a hammer gun, this 16 bore, No. 3916, by Perrins & Son of Broad Street, Worcester, is, in fact, hammerless. The 'hammers' are manual cocking devices and were probably intended to give a clear visual indication in the interest of safety. (Christies)

153 and 154. This 9mm, double-barrelled, hammer gun bears Liège proof marks, but its purpose is not at all clear. It has two independently mounted barrels whose angle relative to the stock can be adjusted by the ring lever mounted beneath the stock. The maximum angle that can be set is 30° and the gun has only a single trigger with manual ejection and Flobert-style locking breeches. The trigger guard is marked SCURIMOBILE NO. 80 and the lugs are inscribed WELT PATENT. (Christies)

155. Charles Lancaster, a leading gunmaker, produced this 20 bore four-barrel gun with 28in Damascus barrels. This is No. 5026, one of only five known.

156. A 16 bore, three-barrel gun, No.

6650, by Edwinson Green & Sons, the third barrel situated above the two side by side. The three-barrel gun, known as a drilling, is popular on the Continent, but it is usually a combination weapon with one rifled and two smooth-bore barrels. This gun has a single trigger to operate all barrels.

157. A 12 bore, sidelock ejector, Greener gun, No. 60530, made in about 1912. As is common with Greener guns, it has no chequering on the grip. The lock plate is chiselled with sporting vignettes.

158. A fine, Holland & Holland Magnum Royal, hammerless, double rifle, detachable sidelock ejector, Magnum .375in flanged rifle. An indicator shows whether the action is cocked and ready to fire.

159. A double-barrelled .303in, sidelock, non-ejector, self-opening game rifle, No. 15108, by J. Purdey & Sons, with 24½in barrels of Whitworth fluid-pressed steel. The rifle is proved for black powder.

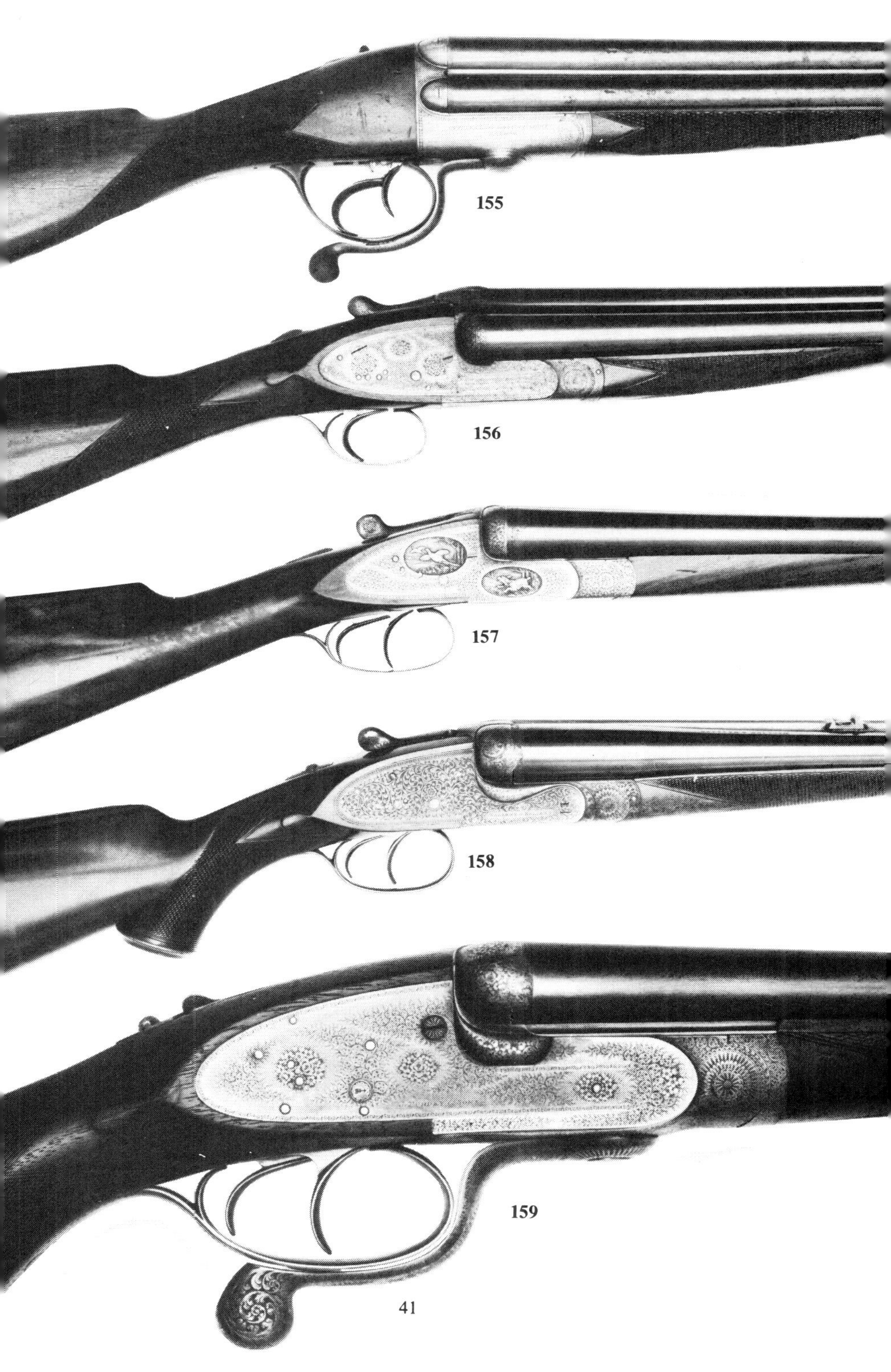

155

156

157

158

159

41

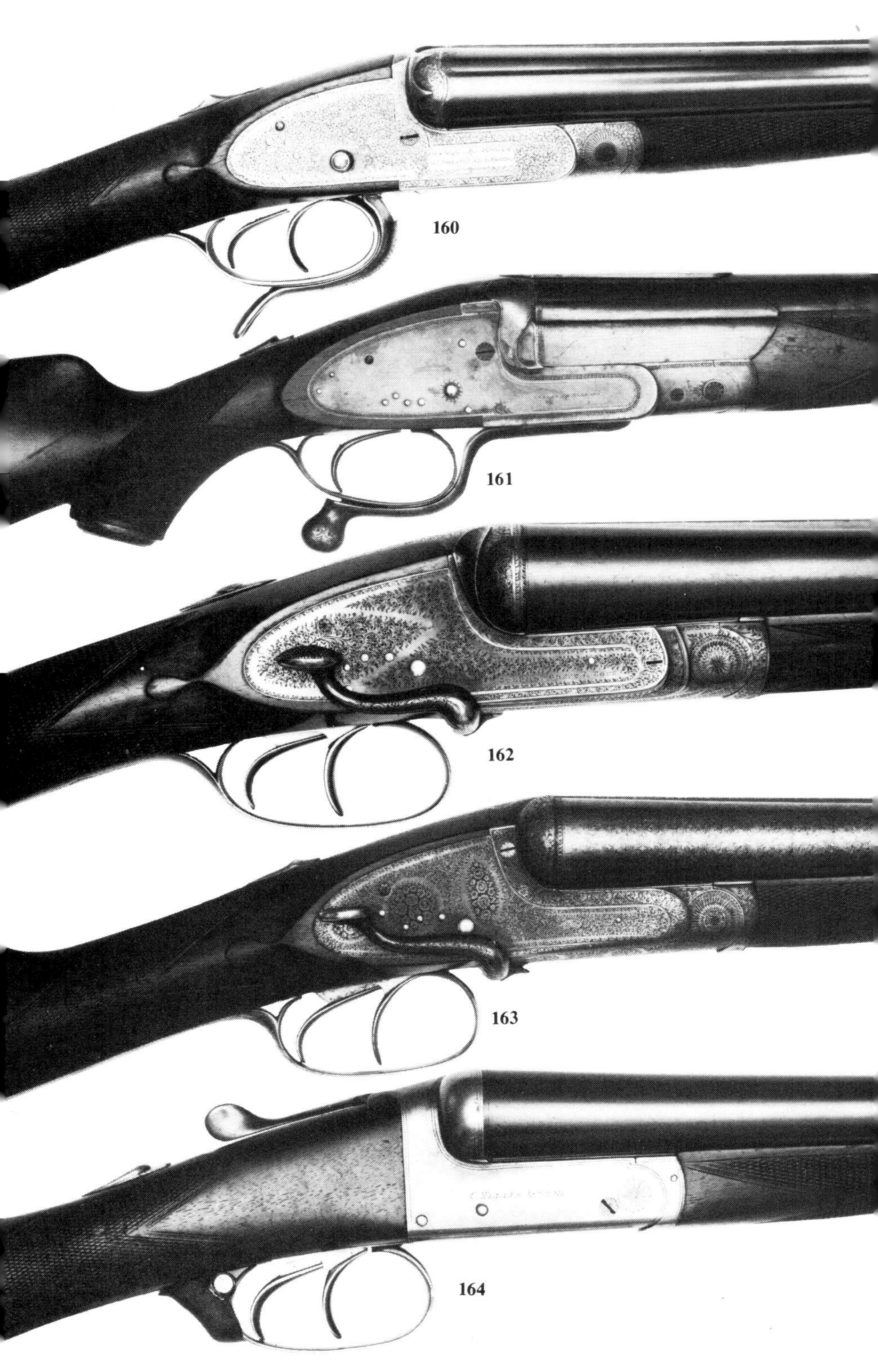

160

161

162

163

164

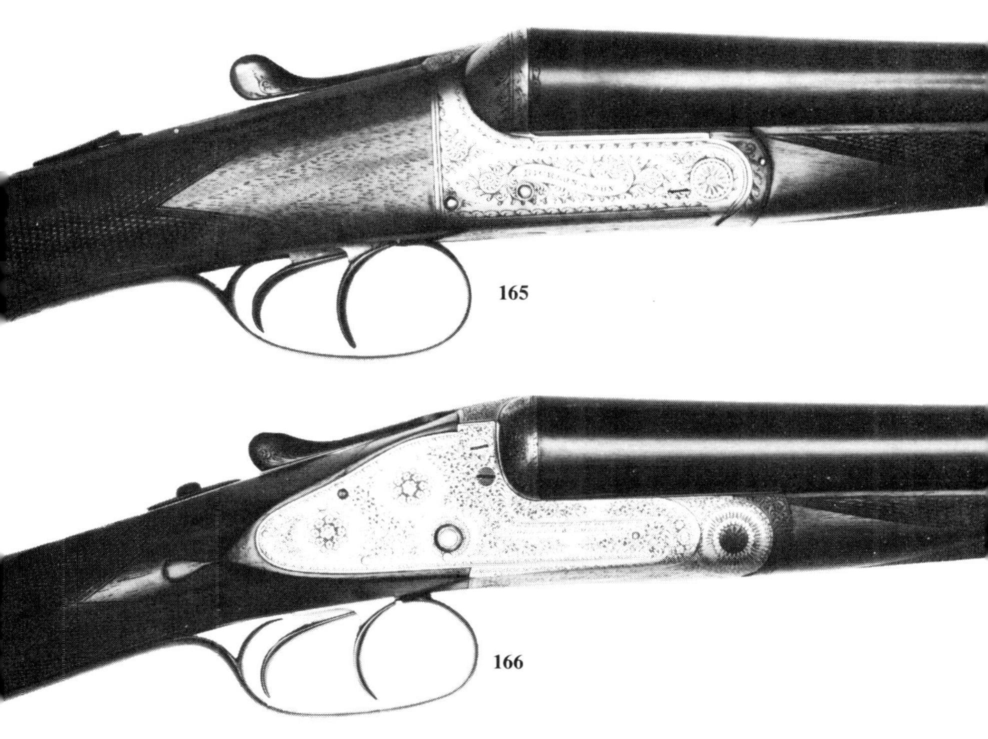

165

166

160. Made by J. Woodward & Sons, with finely engraved sidelocks, this gun is one of a pair of 'Automatic Model' 12 bore guns Nos. 4368–9. It has Whitworth fluid-pressed steel barrels and opens by means of the push-down under-lever.

161. A 4 bore, hammerless, non-ejector wildfowling gun, No. 20053, by Holland & Holland, the lockplates having a minimum of engraving. The breech has a short sighting rib.

162. A 12 bore, double-barrelled, side-lever, sidelock ejector, sporting gun, No. 6758, by Stephen Grant & Sons, with 29in Whitworth barrels. Tang fitted with sliding safety catch; lever and lock finely engraved with foliate scrolls.

163. Finely marked Damascus barrels, with top grade engraving mark this 12 bore, sidelock ejector gun, No. 4104, by Boss & Co., as typical of this outstanding gunmaker. The barrels are opened by a side-lever, a style which did not remain popular for long.

164. A 12 bore, double-barrelled, boxlock, ejector sporting gun, No. 3328, by Charles Hellis & Sons, with 28in barrels, the rib inscribed THE RELIABLE. Top lever opening, tang safety catch, chequered at fore-end and grip, but the lock plain.

165. A 12 bore, double-barrelled, boxlock ejector sporting gun, No. 14029, by John Dickson & Son. The plate has foliate scroll engraved decoration and the maker's name in a ribbon. Chequered stock and tang safety catch.

166. A 12 bore, double-barrelled, Holland & Holland First Model ejector sporting gun, No. 12410. The leg o'mutton lockplate is larger than on most guns and of slightly unusual shape.

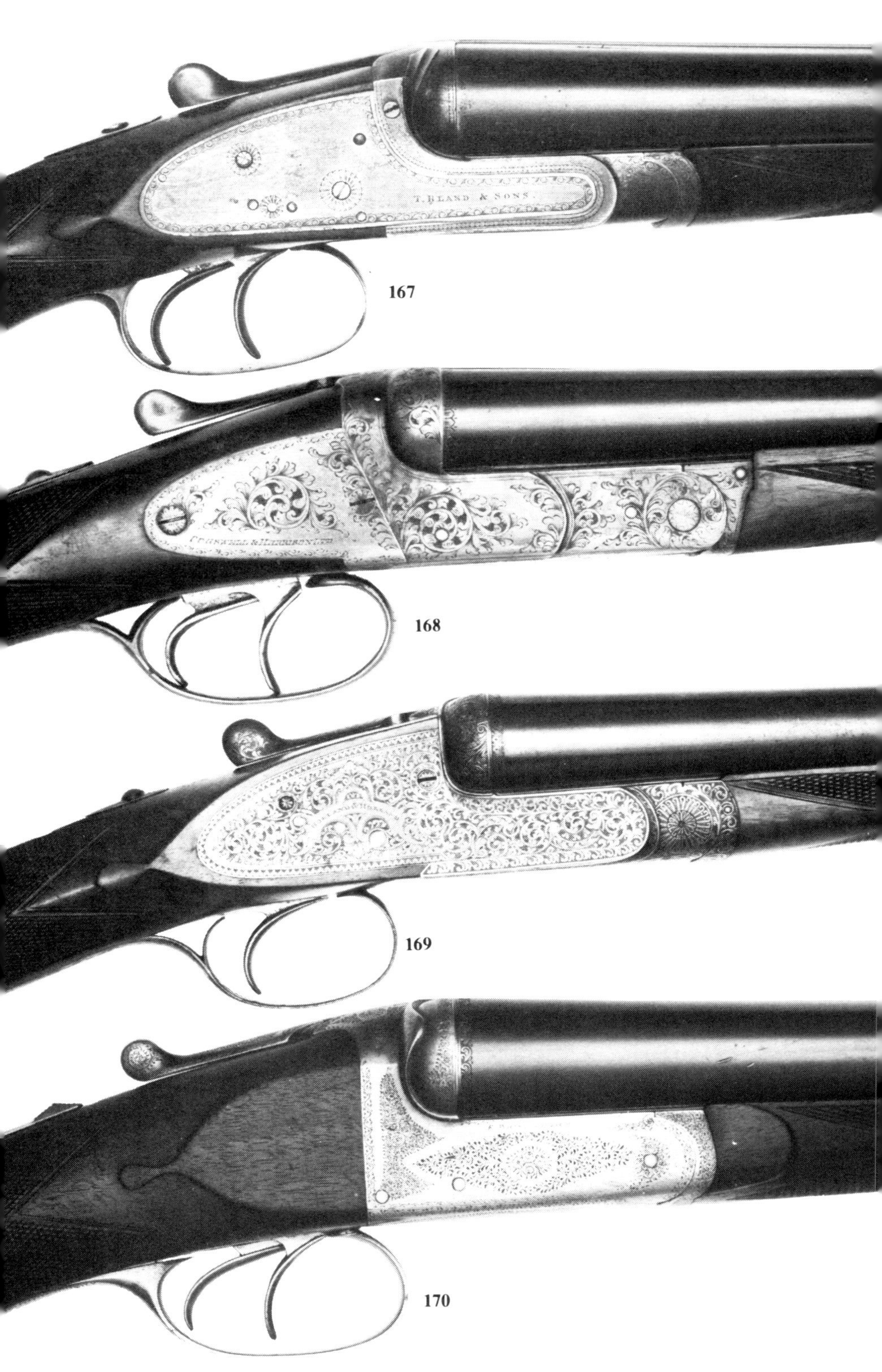
T. BLAND & SONS.
167
CRASWELL & HARRISON LTD
168
169
170

167. A 12 bore, double-barrelled ejector sporting gun, No. 14307, by T. Bland & Sons, the side plates having a minimum of engraved decoration. The barrels have been well used and because of the wear and tear they have been sleeved, in effect given a new lining.

168. A 20 bore double-barrelled, boxlock ejector sporting gun, No. 57392, by Cogswell and Harrison Ltd. It has 27⅜in barrels and the engraving is large and relatively simple in style. Although a boxlock, the weapon is fitted with dummy sideplates.

169. One of a pair of 12 bore, double-barrelled, sidelock, ejector guns, Nos. 22136 and 22550 by Holland & Holland. They are single trigger guns with 30in barrels and the top levers are inlaid 1 and 2 in gold. The locks are profusely engraved with foliate scrolls.

170. An 8 bore, double-barrelled, boxlock, non-ejector sporting gun, No. 23006, by E. Whistler & Co., but with Cogswell and Harrison barrels. The gun may have been made with these barrels, but it is more likely that the original barrels were either out-of-proof or damaged in some way and replaced by this pair.

171. Late nineteenth century engraving of a shooting-party with driven game. The party have hammer guns and behind them stand their loaders whose job it was to keep the sportsmen supplied with ready guns.

171

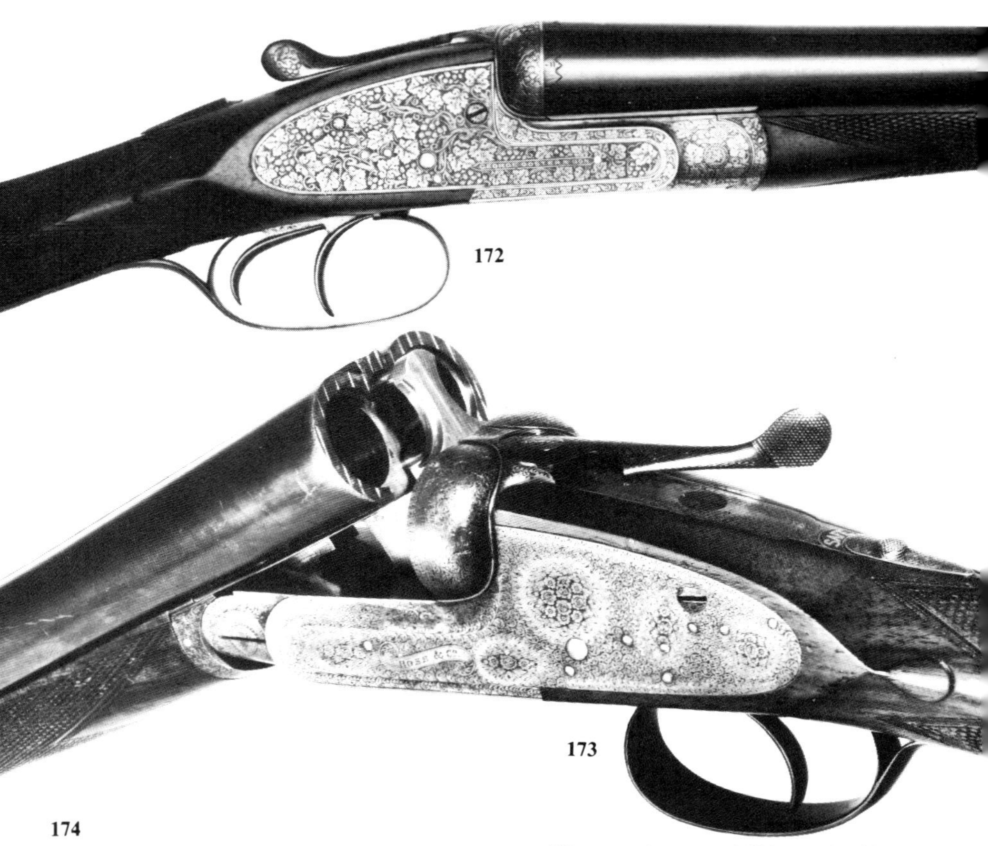

172. One of a pair of 12 bore, double-barrelled, sidelock, ejector sporting guns, No. 1905, by George Coster & Son, decorated with engraved vine leaves and grapes. Stock with chequering at grip and fore-end and tang-mounted push-on safety catch.

173. Detail of the breech and action of a top lever, sidelock, ejector 12 bore by Boss & Co. On the right is the safety catch conveniently placed for operation by the thumb. As the barrels are lowered the ejectors are standing clear of the breech face.

174. Bill for a top quality non self-opening Royal Model gun by Holland & Holland in 1904 – price including cleaning gear and case with initials, £74.14.0d. (£74.70) cash or £83.0.9d. (£83.03) credit. Such a gun with its case as described is today worth £6000–7000 or without its case, £4000–5000. (Holland & Holland)

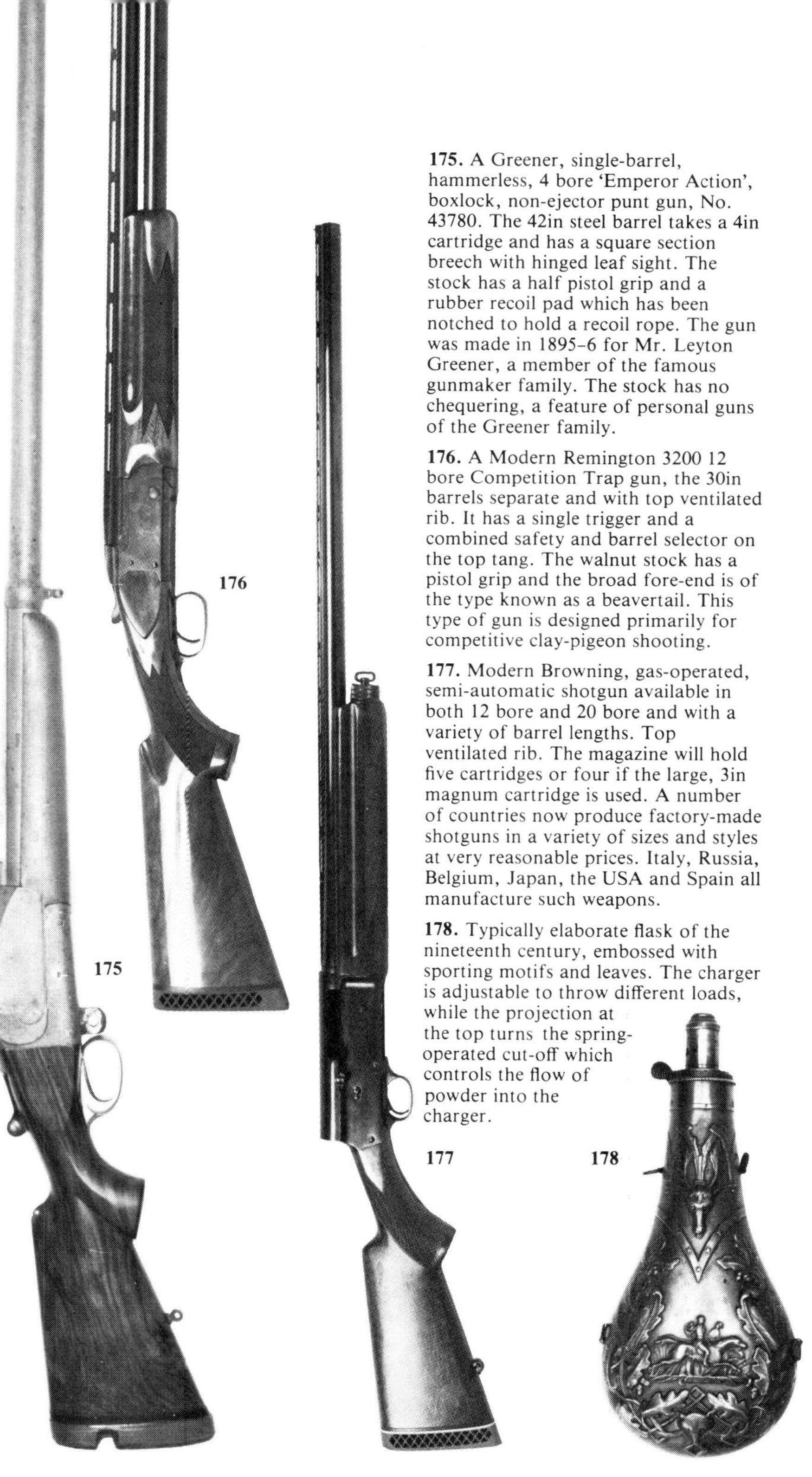

175. A Greener, single-barrel, hammerless, 4 bore 'Emperor Action', boxlock, non-ejector punt gun, No. 43780. The 42in steel barrel takes a 4in cartridge and has a square section breech with hinged leaf sight. The stock has a half pistol grip and a rubber recoil pad which has been notched to hold a recoil rope. The gun was made in 1895–6 for Mr. Leyton Greener, a member of the famous gunmaker family. The stock has no chequering, a feature of personal guns of the Greener family.

176. A Modern Remington 3200 12 bore Competition Trap gun, the 30in barrels separate and with top ventilated rib. It has a single trigger and a combined safety and barrel selector on the top tang. The walnut stock has a pistol grip and the broad fore-end is of the type known as a beavertail. This type of gun is designed primarily for competitive clay-pigeon shooting.

177. Modern Browning, gas-operated, semi-automatic shotgun available in both 12 bore and 20 bore and with a variety of barrel lengths. Top ventilated rib. The magazine will hold five cartridges or four if the large, 3in magnum cartridge is used. A number of countries now produce factory-made shotguns in a variety of sizes and styles at very reasonable prices. Italy, Russia, Belgium, Japan, the USA and Spain all manufacture such weapons.

178. Typically elaborate flask of the nineteenth century, embossed with sporting motifs and leaves. The charger is adjustable to throw different loads, while the projection at the top turns the spring-operated cut-off which controls the flow of powder into the charger.

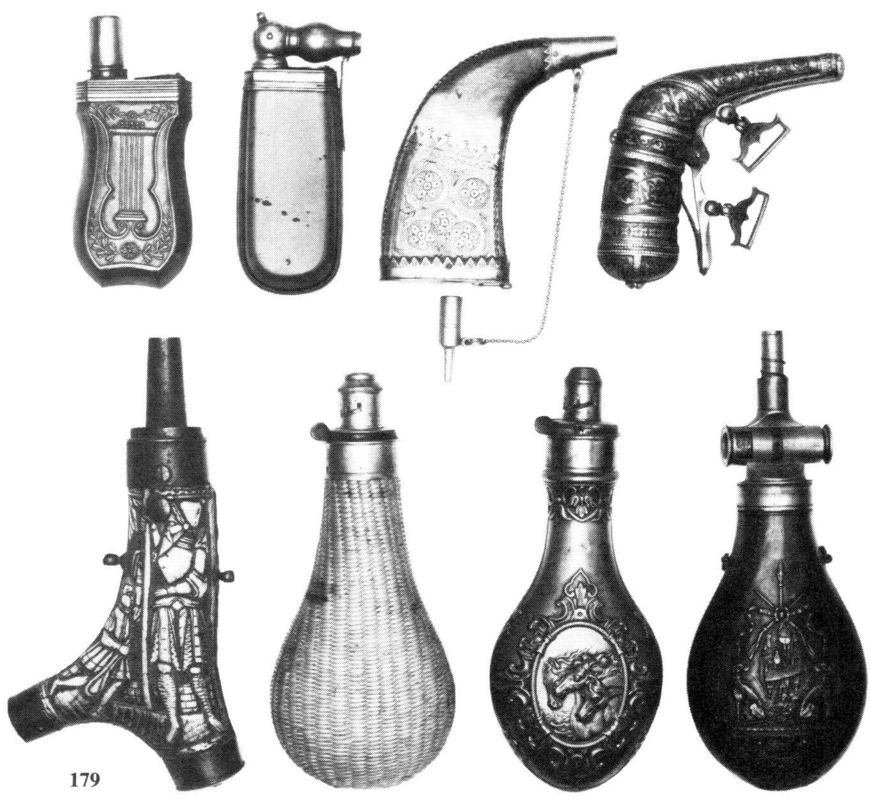

179. A wide-ranging selection of powder flasks from the sixteenth to the nineteenth centuries. Top right: oriental, decorated with silver niello work. Bottom left: seventeenth century, fashioned from a section of antler; next to it is a wicker-covered nineteenth-century flask.

180. A French double-barrelled, percussion-cap sporting gun, the breech inlaid LEPAGE FRES A PAGE with gold, the rib, LECLERC. Gold inlaid locks, half stock. Nineteenth century.

181. Japanese matchlock, octagonal barrel with brass, copper and silver decoration. Nineteenth century.

182. Double-barrelled, flintlock sporting gun by Henry Nock, platinum vent, circa 1810.

183. Scottish percussion-cap sporting rifle, No. 5767, twist barrel with two-groove rifling, flat marked EDINBURGH, barlock signed MORTIMER. Walnut stock, the patchbox engraved COUNTY ARCHERY AND RIFLE CLUB FOR THE WEST OF SCOTLAND. Circa 1850.

184. It was common practice for cartridge manufacturers to use glass cases to display their products. This example is a late one, about 1950, from a French cartridge manufacturer and shows the range of ammunition and components available. A few rifled slug cartridges are shown at the base of the display.

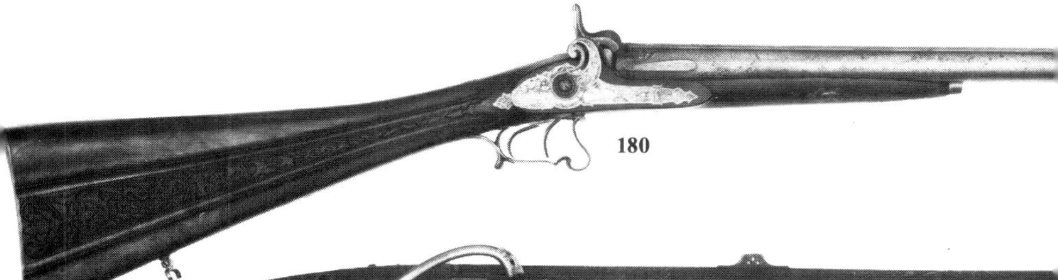

180

181

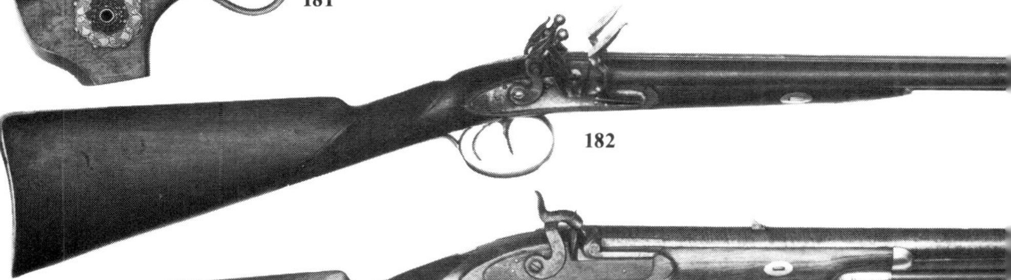

182

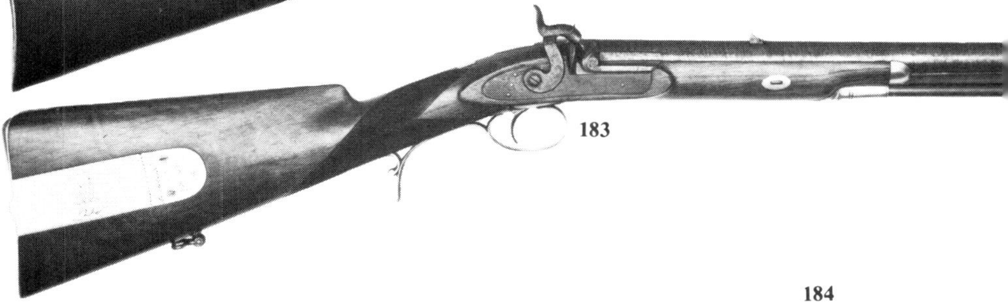

183

184

185

186

185. A range of sporting gun cartridges, from the smallest .22 shot up to the enormous punt-gun cases. The body material was usually card, now plastic is used for the common cartridges. Those cases designed to be reloaded were sometimes made of thin brass. (Holland & Holland)

186. A selection of rifle cartridges including the large big-game express loads designed for use against elephant and rhino. Calibres for hunting were numerous and were designed for general all-purpose hunting or for specific quarry. (Holland & Holland)

187. Reloading machinery (left) made by James Dixon & Sons of Sheffield. The box-like frame holds 12 bore cartridge cases and is passed through the shot-hopper and ramming press, both of which are adjustable for quantities of shot. The hand-held clay pigeon thrower is operated by its heavy, single-coil spring – such a device, despite its slowness, affords opportunities for a much greater variety of angles and heights for the clays.

188. A similar set of reloading machinery for 12 bore cartridges with the tray in position. This set is stamped DIXON & SIMPSON PATENT NO. 39 0 MARCH 16 1887. The decoy duck is carved from a solid block of wood and has inset glass eyes and two mooring rings.

189. Climax patent cartridge-loading gear patented in 1887, Patent No. 3970, with two hoppers, one for powder and the other for shot. (Christies)

190 and 191. An example of the best of English guns – a Holland & Holland De Luxe 12 bore, exhibited in San Francisco in 1971. The superb engraving and gold inlay is the work of a master craftsman, Ken Hunt. (Holland & Holland)

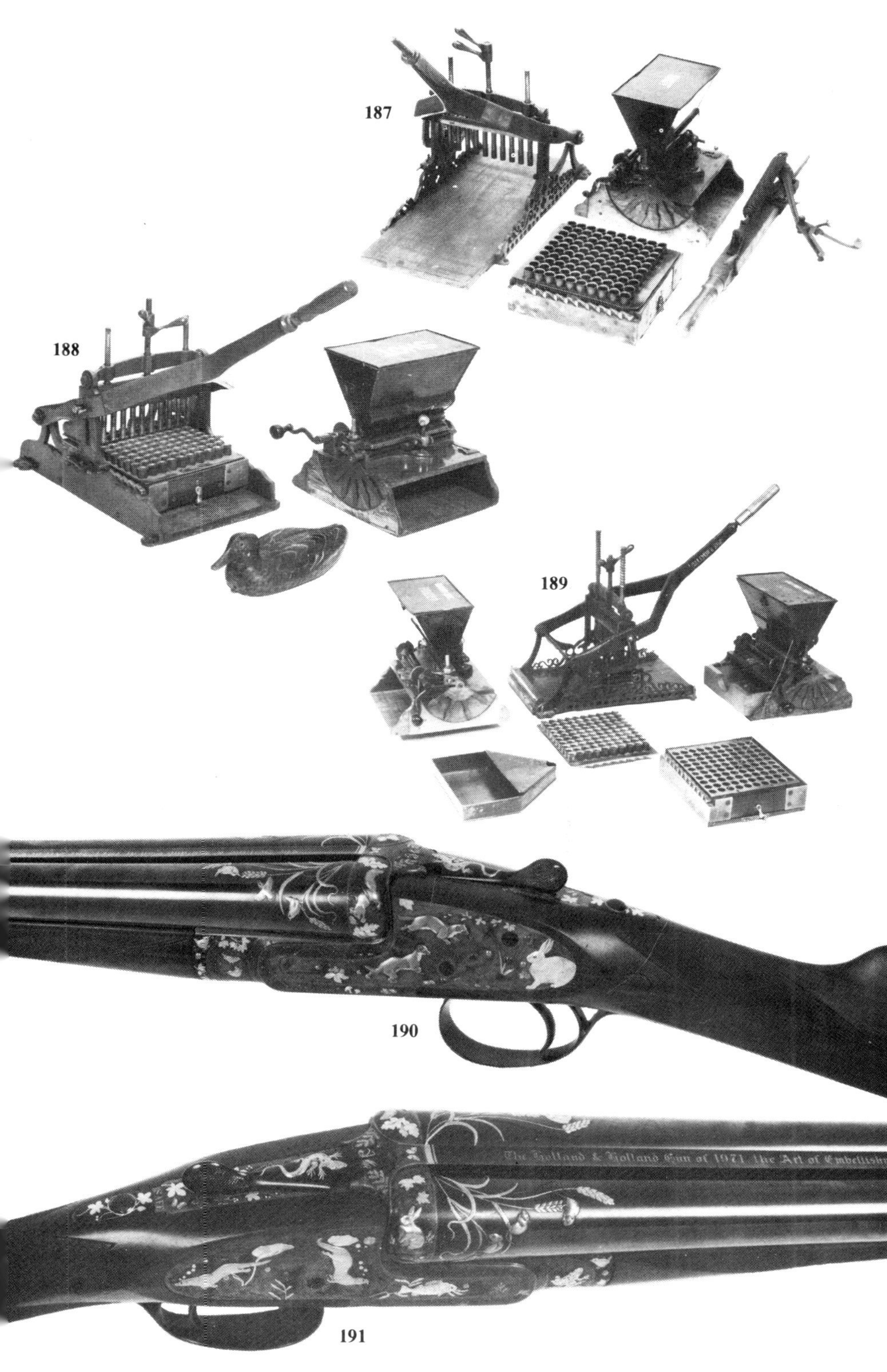

187
188
189
190
The Holland & Holland Gun of 1971 the Art of Embellish
191

192 and 193. A Westley Richards cut-away double-barrelled, hammerless, top lever gun with detachable locks. The floor plate is shown open with action displaying a typical 'whorl' pattern on the polished metal. (Holland & Holland)

194. An unusual 'extra' on a Purdey hammer gun, a top lever gun, No. 13183, is this built-in game counter (The Gallwey). The number of total bag is adjusted by turning the knurled wheel.

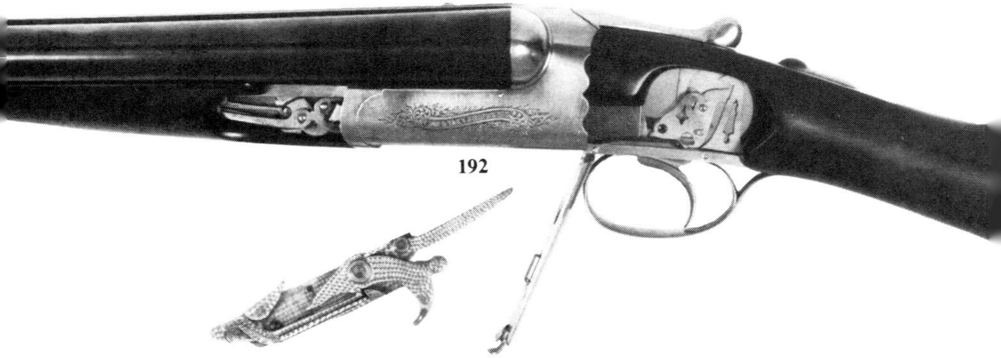

192

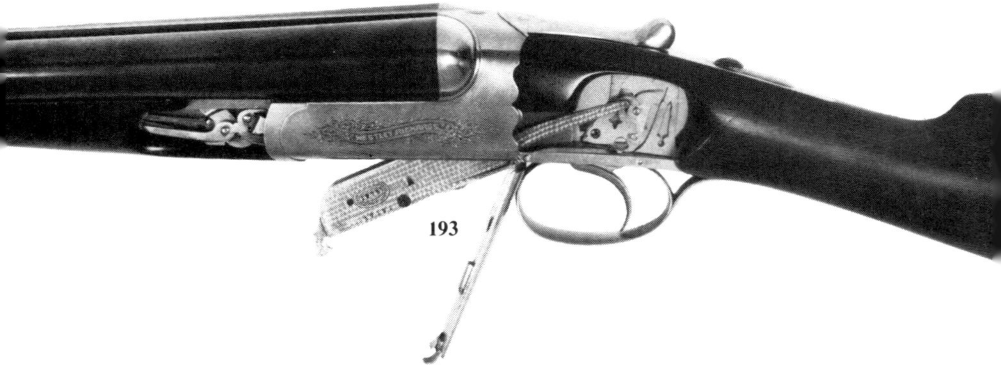

193

194